Revelation Unlocking the Mysteries of the End Times

Bruce BICKEL
&
Stan JANTZ

HARVEST HOUSE™ PUBLISHERS

EUGENE, OREGON

Unless otherwise indicated all Scripture verses are taken from the *Holy Bible,* New Living Translation, copyright ©1996. Used by permission of Tyndale House Publishers, Inc., Wheaton, Illinois 60189, U.S.A. All rights reserved.

Verses marked KJV are taken from the King James Version of the Bible.

Cover by Left Coast Design, Portland, Oregon

Cover photo by Digital Stock: Stormchaser

Harvest House Publishers, Inc. is the exclusive licensee of the trademark, CHRISTIANITY 101.

REVELATION: UNLOCKING THE MYSTERIES OF THE END TIMES
Copyright © 2003 by Bruce Bickel and Stan Jantz
Published by Harvest House Publishers
Eugene, Oregon 97402

Library of Congress Cataloging-in-Publication Data

Bickel, Bruce, 1952–
    Revelation: unlocking the mysteries of the end times / Bruce Bickel and Stan Jantz.
        p. cm. — (Christianity 101™)
    ISBN 0-7369-0794-7 (pbk.)
        1. Bible. N.T. Revelation—Commentaries. 2. Bible. N.T. Revelation—Study and
    teaching. I. Jantz, Stan, 1952– II. Title. III. Series.
    BS2825.53 .B53 2003
    228'.07—dc21

                                                                          2002010618

Printed in the United States of America.

        04   05   06   07   08   09   10   11 / DP-KB / 10   9   8   7   6   5   4   3   2

Contents

A Note from the Authors

*W*e don't know you, but we do know at least three things about you:

- You are a curious person.

- You love an adventure.

- You are interested in the end times.

Okay, so it didn't take a couple of geniuses to figure that out. The very fact that you have picked up this study on the book of Revelation tells us at least that much. Beyond that, we suspect that you have some sort of goal in mind as you begin this study. Even curious and adventurous people need a goal. They don't just start something challenging unless they know they can finish it with a sense of accomplishment.

The same is true of your study of Revelation. You don't want to simply go through the motions of learning about the mysterious symbolism and the prophetic events you've heard about since you were a kid. No, you have a goal in mind. Whatever that goal is, we urge you to write it down in the margin of this page or inside the front cover of this book. Just in case you can't articulate your goal right now, we've got one we think works pretty well for this book. Here it is:

> The reason you should study the book of Revelation is to grow closer to Jesus and to develop a hunger for His return.

Just a Little Help

The last thing the world needs is another commentary on Revelation. That's why we have taken a different approach in *Revelation: Unlocking the Mysteries of the End Times*. There are lots of scholarly books that will give you the technical theological concepts and the prophetic timetables of the book of Revelation. If you want to dig into the original language of John's letter to the seven churches, you can find a commentary that will bring out the meanings of the Greek words. But if you simply want a little something to help you understand Revelation and what it means to you personally, then this is the book you need to read.

Our approach to Bible study is very simple. We won't get in the way of your own personal study, but we will guide and encourage you along the way. In the first two chapters of this study, we will explain the historical, cultural, and theological settings for Revelation. We'll give you the central focus and the major themes of the book. In the other eleven chapters, we will walk through Revelation with you (okay, so it will probably be more like a *run* through Revelation), helping you to understand what it means—and what it means to *you*.

Christianity 101™ Bible Studies

This Bible study on Revelation is part of a series called Christianity 101™ Bible Studies. We've designed this series to combine the biblical content of a commentary with the life applications of a Bible study. By reading this book and answering the questions, you will learn the basics of what you need to know so you will get more meaning from the Bible. Not only that, but you will be able to apply what the Bible says to your everyday Christian life.

And just in case you want even more help in your study of God's Word, we have listed some books that were helpful to us in our study of Revelation. You'll find these at the end of the book in a section called "Dig Deeper." In addition, we have put together an online resource exclusively for users of the Christianity 101™ Bible Studies. All you have to do is click on www.christianity101online.com (see page 175 for details).

This Book Is for You

Maybe this is your first time using a resource for studying the Bible, or maybe you are an experienced Bible student. Either way, we think this book is for you if...

- Reading the Bible is sometimes a little confusing for you. You get the overall picture, but you want additional information and insights to help you better understand how the Bible fits into your life and the world around you.

- You enjoy reading the Bible, but you don't think you're getting enough out of it. Sometimes the Bible seems like a history book or a collection of wise sayings. Because you believe the Bible is the living Word of God, you want it to change the way you live.

- You and a few friends want to study a book of the Bible together, and you figure Revelation is a good place to start. (You're a very brave person, by the way.) You don't want a Bible study that will force you all to come to the same conclusions. You want a book that will give everyone room to think for themselves.

A Few Suggestions Before You Begin

As you read this book, we ask only one thing of you. Have your Bible open to Revelation so we can do this together. Remember, we aren't your teachers. We are more like trail guides explaining a few things and showing you some points of interest along the way. The Holy Spirit is your teacher, and He's the best there is. He will show you everything you need to know about Revelation and how it applies to your Christian life.

But we know these things because God has revealed them to us by his Spirit, and his Spirit searches out everything and shows us even God's deep secrets (1 Corinthians 2:10).

God will speak directly to you through His Word and through the inner voice of the Holy Spirit. Our prayer is that your study of this exciting and sometimes mysterious book will change your life as you grow closer to Jesus and better understand God's plan for the ages.

If You Are Studying Revelation on Your Own

- Pray and ask God to help you understand His Word.

- Before you begin, read Revelation all the way through to get an overview. Don't worry if you don't understand much right now.

- As you work through each chapter in this guide, try to understand the themes of Revelation and how they relate to the rest of the Bible.

- Write out your answers to the questions and exercises in the "Study the Word" section at the end of each chapter. Writing down your thoughts will reinforce what you are learning.

- Thank God for the wonderful riches of His Word, for His provision for your life now, and for His plans for your future.

If You Are Studying Revelation in a Group

- Prepare for the Bible study by following all our suggestions for studying Revelation on your own.

- Be a willing participant in the discussion but don't dominate the conversation.

- Encourage and affirm the other people in your group as they talk.

- Be open and honest in your answers. In you don't understand something, say so! Someone else may have the answer you're looking for.

- Sharing what a particular passage means to you is okay, but first you should try to discover what it means to everyone. Remember, biblical truths aren't different for different people.

- If someone shares something confidential, keep it in the group. At the same time, avoid turning your group Bible study into a gossip session.

- Pray for the other members of your group on a regular basis. Here's how Paul prayed for a group of Christians in his day:

So we have continued praying for you ever since we first heard about you. We ask God to give you a complete understanding of what he wants to do in your lives, and we ask him to make you wise with spiritual wisdom. Then the way you live will always honor and please the Lord, and you will continually do good, kind things for others. All the while, you will learn to know God better and better (Colossians 1:9-10).

That's our prayer for you as well. So let's get started.

Chapter 1

No one can shut his eyes to the difficulty of
the Revelation. It is the most difficult book
in the Bible; but it is infinitely worth
studying, for it contains the blazing faith of
the Christian Church in the days when life
was an agony and men expected the end of
the heavens and the earth as they knew
them but still believed that beyond the
terror was the glory and above the raging of
men was the power of God.

—*William Barclay*

When we first began to research and write this study on Revelation, we were intimidated. How could we, a couple of Bible amateurs, adequately understand and explain the Bible's most mysterious book? Then we realized that we were putting the emphasis in the wrong place. We were trying to understand every detail and explain each shade of meaning without first looking at the overall picture.

Imagine viewing a beautiful painting from a distance of six inches. You can see the brush strokes and individual colors, but you get an incomplete (and not very pretty) perspective because you miss the big picture. You can't appreciate the full beauty of the painting until you step back and take it all in.

That's what we're going to do in this chapter—step back and look at Revelation in the context of *how, when,* and *why* it was written.

A Book for the Ages

*T*he book of Revelation has a strange effect on people. Either it puzzles them so much that they stay away from it like the plague or it fascinates them so much that they can't get enough. Why does Revelation seem to excite people as much as it troubles them? Consider a few elements of Revelation. In its 22 chapters and 404 verses, Revelation contains...

- strange creatures and mysterious symbolism
- portrayals of a terrible time of judgment

- glimpses of a horrible place called hell

- descriptions of a beautiful place called heaven

- a comprehensive portrait of the Almighty One, Jesus Christ

Studying the book of Revelation takes you to another world. It's like watching the greatest science-fiction movie ever—only this isn't science and it's not fiction. While we may never fully understand what all the symbolism means, we can be sure that the events described in Revelation are very real. Even though we don't know *when* these things will happen, we can be assured that they *will* happen because the same God who created the universe and got everything going in the first place has a plan for its conclusion. And His plan involves *you,* someone He loves very much.

So why should you study the book of Revelation? Here are seven good reasons (as you're going to find out, *seven* is a popular number in Revelation).

Seven Good Reasons to Study Revelation

1. Revelation is the last book of the Bible.

What good is any book unless there's a final chapter? The Bible would be incomplete without Revelation, and your knowledge of the Scriptures and your appreciation for God and what He has planned for you would be incomplete without a careful study of Revelation.

2. Revelation is the only prophetic book in the New Testament.

The Old Testament includes 17 books of prophecy, but Revelation is the only one in the New Testament. About

2000 of the Bible's 2500 prophecies have already been fulfilled to the letter. The remaining 500—most of which are in the book of Revelation—are unfulfilled. Here's the deal. Because the Bible has been 100 percent correct so far, we can be 100 percent sure that the rest of the Bible's prophecies will also be fulfilled to the letter (even if we don't understand all of the letters).

3. Revelation describes the Second Coming of Christ and the events leading up to it.

The Second Coming of Christ to earth is the centerpiece of Bible prophecy. The Old Testament prophets foretold a time when Jesus would come to earth the first time as the suffering Messiah, but they also looked forward to a second time when Jesus would come as a conquering King. Revelation reveals those events that will take place before, during, and after the Second Coming of Christ. If you get nothing else from the book of Revelation, you need to have a firm grip on the reality of the Second Coming.

4. Revelation explains how Satan, the great enemy of God and humankind, will be finally and forever defeated.

Jesus called Satan "the prince of this world" (John 14:30). The apostle Paul called him "the god of this evil world" (2 Corinthians 4:4). Peter referred to Satan as "your great enemy" (1 Peter 5:8). Satan has a great influence in the world, but he can never win the ultimate battle against God and His people. No matter how much damage he does, he is doomed to defeat. That should be a great comfort to us as we confront Satan and his forces of evil.

5. Even though Revelation talks mainly about events that haven't yet happened, the message is relevant for us today.

Many Christians make the mistake of assuming that Revelation is only about the future, and therefore it doesn't have much practical application for daily living. As you are going to find out, Revelation has a message we can apply right now.

6. God promises to bless anyone who reads Revelation and obeys what it says.

This reason alone should be enough to read and study Revelation. No other book in the Bible comes with this kind of promise.

7. The theme of Revelation is Jesus Christ.

This is the most important thing to know about Revelation and the most compelling reason to study the book: It's all about Jesus. The four Gospels present the story of Jesus living His life as a human on earth, but they don't give us the total picture. Here in Revelation we see the complete revelation of Jesus in all His glory.

Who Wrote Revelation?

This isn't a big mystery because the author identifies himself within the first few verses: "This letter is from John" (1:4). The traditional view is that this is the apostle John, who was one of the original 12 disciples. This is the same John who wrote the fourth biography of Jesus (called the Gospel of John) as well as the three New Testament letters that bear his name (1, 2, and 3 John).

$\mathcal{R}$evelation at a $\mathcal{G}$lance

Author:	the apostle John
Date written:	A.D. 95
Written to:	seven churches in Asia Minor and believers everywhere
Type of book:	a prophetic book written in the style of apocalyptic literature
Setting:	John wrote Revelation while in exile on the island of Patmos. Churches and Christians at the end of the first century were experiencing intense persecution at the hands of Emperor Domitian and other Roman authorities.
Purpose:	to offer hope and encouragement to persecuted believers and to convict believers living in compromise with the world
Major themes:	The major theme of Revelation is Jesus Christ. Other themes include the sovereignty of God, the lordship of Jesus, the Second Coming of Jesus, the perseverance of believers, the judgment of evil by God, and our hope in Christ.

John wrote Revelation while exiled on the island of Patmos, a small, rocky island located in the Aegean Sea about 50 miles from the city of Ephesus (in present-day Turkey). The Romans established Patmos as a kind of criminal colony, so the Roman emperor Domitian banished John to Patmos "for preaching the word of God and speaking about Jesus" (1:9), which was illegal under Domitian's reign. On this desolate, "God forsaken" place, Jesus revealed Himself in all His glory and showed John the dramatic events of the end of the age.

John the Apostle: One Tough Customer

The Roman authorities considered John to be an effective and therefore dangerous leader of the Christian church, which they were persecuting. According to *Foxe's Book of Martyrs,* the Romans arrested John in Ephesus and sent him to Rome, where they tried to boil him alive in oil. When he emerged unharmed, the emperor Domitian banished John to Patmos. After Domitian's death, John returned to Ephesus, where he died of natural causes in A.D. 98. John was the only one of the 12 apostles who wasn't martyred for his faith in Jesus.

What Was Going On?

Most Bible scholars believe that John wrote Revelation around A.D. 95, near the end of Domitian's reign. To understand what was going on at this time, you have to understand something about Domitian and his enforcement of Caesar worship. The rulers of the Roman Empire were given the title "Caesar" as a tribute to Julius Caesar, the first and most famous Caesar of all and Rome's greatest monarch. He laid the foundation for the Roman imperial system.

The worship of the emperor, or Caesar worship, began after Julius Caesar died in 44 B.C. As the Roman Empire flourished, the citizens of Rome saw themselves as pretty special. Believing the ruler of Rome was a god wasn't too much of a stretch for them. Besides, adding another god to their pantheon wasn't that big a deal for the Romans. Like the Greeks, the Romans actively worshiped the gods of mythology.

Although all of the Caesars who ruled in the first century tolerated the worship given to them, not all of them were comfortable with it. They allowed the Jews—and later the Christians—to worship their God rather than Caesar. The exceptions to this benevolence were Caligula (who ruled in A.D. 32–41) and Domitian (A.D. 81–96), who enforced the worship they thought they deserved. Caligula was basically insane. He died before he had the chance to place his own image in the Holy of Holies in the Temple in Jerusalem (a really bad idea). Domitian, on the other hand, was sane, but he was pure evil. William Barclay calls him a "cold-blooded persecutor" who actually believed he was a god. He *demanded* Caesar worship and began a "campaign of bitter persecution" against anyone who refused to worship him. In particular, he targeted Jews and Christians.

$\mathcal{P}$ersecution in the $\mathcal{T}$wenty-$\mathcal{F}$irst $\mathcal{C}$entury

Those of us who live in the West in the twenty-first century enjoy the freedom to worship God openly and actively. But we should never take this privilege for granted. Just because you can go to church and have a Bible study in your home anytime you want doesn't mean the rest of the world operates by the same standard. In many countries, professing faith in Jesus is illegal, and in more places than you can imagine, people are being martyred for their faith (*martyr* is a name given to anyone put to death for his or her beliefs). According to The Voice of the Martyrs, an estimated 165,000 people were martyred for believing in Jesus in various parts of the world in the year 2000.

To Whom Was Revelation Written?

There are two audiences for this remarkable book. First are "the seven churches in the province of Asia" (1:4). Located in what is now southwestern Turkey, these churches were familiar to John, who knew their strengths and weaknesses. The other audience is Christians everywhere and for all time (1:3). The message of Revelation is as relevant for us today as it was to Christians at the end of the first century.

Why Was Revelation Written?

Revelation was written for three main reasons:

1. Revelation was written to encourage the churches and the Christians facing Roman persecution.

In this regard, Revelation is a book of hope. No matter how bad things seem and no matter how bad things might get, we need to set our eyes on Jesus, "who loves us and has freed us from our sins by shedding his blood for us" (1:5). Soon this same Jesus will come again "with the clouds of heaven" (1:7) to conquer sin, Satan, and death, and to make all things new.

2. Revelation was written to address the spiritual complacency of Christians.

As we're going to see in chapter 5, Jesus came down hard on Christians who were "neither hot nor cold." He told them:

> But since you are like lukewarm water, I will spit you out of my mouth! (3:16).

As much as Revelation encourages the persecuted church, it is a wake-up call for a complacent and compromising church.

3. Revelation was written to deliver the harshest of warnings to a rebellious world.

A time of judgment that will shake the world to its very foundation is coming. Although Bible scholars disagree on the details, the sequence, and the timing of the events foretold in Revelation, they agree on this important point: Jesus is coming back, and when He does, God will judge the world and punish sin—for good. In this way Revelation is like a ticking clock whose alarm could go off anytime.

As you can see, Revelation was written for all people. If you are a Christian, it is your *book of hope.* If you are a Christian living in compromise, it is a *book of conviction.* And if you are someone who has chosen to reject Christ altogether, it is a *book of warning.*

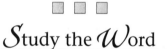

$\mathcal{S}$tudy the $\mathcal{W}$ord

1. Review the seven good reasons to study Revelation. Which one is most motivating to you? Why?

2. In preparation for this study, ask yourself (and answer) these questions:

   • Do I really believe the world is headed for mass destruction?

   • Do I really believe Satan and his helpers will lead many people astray as the end draws near?

- Do I really believe Jesus Christ will physically and triumphantly return to the earth?

  - Do I really believe God will help me remain faithful to the end?

3. Why might God have chosen John to receive the Revelation?

4. Why have Christians been objects of persecution for 2000 years?

5. Does the emperor worship of ancient Rome have any modern counterparts?

6. Why might people be so hostile to Jesus Christ and His followers?

7. As a Christian living in a country where you can freely worship Jesus, what can you do to help persecuted Christians in other parts of the world?

Chapter 2

Although many details in Revelation...are debatable, the basic thrust is not. The true and living God summons us from our preoccupation with the world to recognize, in light of his ultimate plan for history, what really matters and what really does not.

—*Craig S. Keener*

For nearly two millennia people have been debating the meaning of Revelation, and we're still debating to this day. We want so badly to figure God out, but we have to realize that God may have intentionally left some of the contents of this great book under a cloud of mystery. Don't let that bother you or keep you from searching out the things you can know. Remember, God is a God you can know, but He is also a God of mystery. "'My thoughts are completely different from yours,' says the LORD. 'And my ways are far beyond anything you could imagine'" (Isaiah 55:8). Rather than worrying about the things God has chosen to keep to Himself, concentrate on the things He has clearly shown us.

In this chapter we're going to set the stage for our study of the book of Revelation. We will look at the various approaches to Revelation and then give you the themes of this great book.

Approaching Revelation

*E*verybody assumes that Revelation is a *prophetic* book, and that's true, but Revelation is also *apocalyptic* in nature. Actually, *apocalypse* means "revelation." Apocalyptic literature is a specific type of Jewish writing that has its roots in Old Testament prophecy. In the Old Testament, a prophet was a spokesman for God to the people of Israel. He gave insight into the mind of God and delivered the literal message of God. So when a true prophet spoke or wrote, he was declaring the message of God to the people.

Old Testament prophets did their share of *foretelling* future events (such as the coming of the Messiah), but they mainly engaged in *telling*. In other words, they protested the current activities of God's people, such as idolatry, injustice, corruption, and complacency. After Malachi, the last Old Testament prophet, wrote his book, God stopped speaking to Israel directly. The hope of God's kingdom, promised by the prophets, began to fade.

Ezekiel, Daniel, and Zechariah all include apocalyptic sections, but most apocalyptic literature was written after Malachi (the last book in the Old Testament). From 200 B.C. to A.D. 100, this form of writing attempted to explain the present evil in the world through symbols, and to give assurance that God would once again intervene in history and eventually usher in His kingdom. Of all the apocalyptic writings of this period, Revelation is the only one that was included in the Bible.

By definition, apocalyptic literature is symbolic. We have to avoid the temptation to interpret each of these symbols too literally or too narrowly, especially in the context of our current knowledge and experience. (For example, we cannot say that the locusts in Revelation 9:7-10 are helicopters.) Apocalyptic writers, including John, never meant for their symbols to be blueprints for future devices. A better way to look at apocalyptic symbolism is to see it as a graphic portrayal of events, beings, or characteristics in the supernatural world.

How Do You Interpret Revelation?

Okay, so Revelation contains a lot of mysterious symbolism. Does that mean we can't interpret any of it? Not at all. At least four different approaches have been used to understand and apply the message of Revelation. Here again, people don't all agree as to which approach is best because each one has its merits. For the purposes of this study on Revelation, we're going to settle on one particular approach, but that doesn't mean that the other three approaches to interpreting Revelation don't have value in certain areas.

---

*E*ssential and *N*onessential

As long as we agree on the essential truths of the Christian faith, we can agree to disagree on some of the nonessential truths. An example of an *essential* truth is believing that Jesus, who is the only way to be saved, will return to earth a second time for those who have trusted Him as their personal Savior. An example of a *nonessential* truth is the timing of Christ's return, or whether all believers dead and alive will be "raptured" before, during, or after the Great Tribulation. One is a salvation issue, while the other is not.

Four Main Approaches to Interpreting Revelation

1. *The Symbolic Approach*

Sometimes called the idealist approach, this view holds that all of Revelation should be interpreted symbolically. The symbols describe the struggle between good and evil that plagues our planet. Strict symbolists believe that none of the symbols in Revelation should be interpreted as real, historic events. Rather, they represent spiritual truth.

Main problem with this view: This interpretation has no focus on actual future events, which leaves no place for the literal Second Coming of Jesus.

2. The Historical Approach

This view was popular with the Reformers (people like Martin Luther and John Calvin). They believed that the prophecies of Revelation coincided with actual historic events from the time of the early church to their own time. Historicists believe that each symbol, creature, and characteristic in Revelation corresponds with a particular historical event or figure.

Main problem with this view: This interpretation changes as history progresses. Consequently, we are left with as many interpretations as interpreters.

3. The Preterist Approach

More popular than the symbolic or historical approach, this view holds that the symbolism in Revelation relates only to the early church. Most of Revelation has nothing to do with the future since it should be interpreted in light of first century events. In other words, all prophecies have already been fulfilled.

Main problem with this view: This interpretation doesn't leave room for future events and unfulfilled prophecy.

4. The Futurist Approach

People who hold this view interpret Revelation like this: The first three chapters apply to the time in which it was written—"the things that are now happening" (1:19). The rest of Revelation deals with events yet to come— "the things that will happen later" (1:19). Events depicted in Revelation, such as the Great Tribulation and the Second Coming, are interpreted as literally as possible.

Main problem with this view: This approach would have been of little comfort to the early church because they would not have understood it.

Our Approach

We want to make it clear that your salvation does not depend on which view of Revelation you choose to hold. You can believe that Christ will come again at some future time to defeat evil, to judge evildoers, and to reward those who have believed in His name with an eternal future, and still hold any view. That said, we believe the futurist approach is the one that is the most practical and the most compatible with the rest of Scripture and the character of God because it allows us to see God working now as well as in the future. As futurists we can...

- Apply what God was saying to the seven churches in Asia to our churches and our lives today. In this way Revelation offers *present guidance* for all believers at any given moment because it tells us about the person of Jesus Christ and shows us how to live for Him right now.

- Understand that God's plan for the consummation of history centers on the person of Jesus and the Second Coming. In this way Revelation offers *future hope* to all believers who have lived in every time period since John wrote his book, especially those who have experienced persecution, because it describes a time when Jesus Christ will defeat sin, Satan, and death once and for all.

The Themes of Revelation

Before we dig into Revelation, we need to step back and get a quick overview. To keep from getting lost in the trees (we'll try not to let that happen), we need to see the forest. We can do this by looking at the themes of Revelation.

We've already said that the major theme of Revelation is Jesus Christ. We've also mentioned other themes, but we haven't talked about them much. Here's a quick survey:

God Is Sovereign

This means He rules over all with absolute authority and power. God's control over His creation is called His *sovereignty.* In Revelation, John wrote:

> *And the twenty-four elders sitting on their thrones before God fell on their faces and worshiped him. And they said, "We give thanks to you, Lord God Almighty, the one who is and who always was, for now you have assumed your great power and have begun to reign"* (11:16-17).

God's sovereignty means that nothing occurs outside of His knowledge, His control, or His will. More than any other book in the Bible, Revelation shows the incomparable power and the incomprehensible love of God, who is directing history for the sake of those who put their trust in Him. We can trust God's sovereignty for the future and take comfort in it now.

Jesus Is Lord

God invaded human history in the person of Jesus 2000 years ago. Jesus did not cling to His rights as God, but rather He humbled Himself by dying a criminal's death for us on the cross. Paul wrote:

> *Because of this, God raised him up to the heights of heaven and gave him a name that is above every other name, so that at the name of Jesus every knee*

will bow, in heaven and on earth and under the earth, and every tongue will confess that Jesus Christ is Lord, to the glory of God the Father (Philippians 2:9-11).

John saw a vision of "thousands and millions of angels around the throne." And they sang:

The Lamb is worthy—the Lamb who was killed. He is worthy to receive power and riches and wisdom and strength and honor and glory and blessing (Revelation 5:12).

Revelation shows the absolute worthiness of our Lord and Savior. He is the one we will worship forever in heaven, and He is the one we can worship now.

Jesus Is Coming Back

While He was still on the earth, Jesus told His disciples that He was going to heaven to prepare a place for them. Then He told them He would return: "When everything is ready, I will come and get you, so that you will always be with me where I am" (John 14:3). Christ's return is a grand theme of Revelation. Near the end of the book, Jesus said:

See, I am coming soon, and my reward is with me, to repay all according to their deeds. I am the Alpha and Omega, the First and the Last, the Beginning and the End (22:12-13).

Jesus spoke these words more than 1900 years ago. That's a long time from our limited, human perspective, but from God's perspective it's nothing (2 Peter 3:8). We don't need to wonder if Jesus is ever going to return. We can be sure that God's timing is perfect. Jesus will come back to earth at just the right moment.

God's People Will Persevere

One of the biggest questions Christians ask is, Can I lose my salvation? The simple answer is that all who are truly saved will continue in the Christian life until death—or until Christ returns—and then they will join Jesus in heaven. In other words, they will persevere to the end. Jesus said: "And this is the will of God, that I should not lose even one of all those he has given me, but that I should raise them to eternal life at the last day" (John 6:39).

If you're a child of God, you will persevere to the end. Nothing can take your salvation away. At the same time, you must be faithful to God no matter what. Someday your perseverance will pay off. John witnessed this amazing sight:

> I heard a loud shout from the throne, saying, "Look, the home of God is now among his people! He will live with them, and they will be his people. God himself will be with them. He will remove all of their sorrows, and there will be no more death or sorrow or crying or pain. For the old world and its evils are gone forever" (Revelation 21:3-4).

Judgment Day Is Coming

According to an old saying, "Nothing is certain except death and taxes." Well, you can add *judgment* to that list. The writer of Hebrews wrote: "And just as it is destined that each person dies only once and after that comes judgment, so also Christ died only once as a sacrifice to take away the sins of many people" (Hebrews 9:27-28). No one can avoid judgment because God is going to judge sin and sinners, and all have sinned (Romans 3:23). Those who have accepted the sacrifice of Christ to take away their sins will be rewarded with eternal life. Those who have rejected Christ will face eternal punishment. John saw this vision:

> *The nations were angry with you, but now the time of your wrath has come. It is time to judge the dead and reward your servants. You will reward your prophets and your holy people, all who fear your name, from the least to the greatest. And you will destroy all who have caused destruction on the earth* (Revelation 11:18).

Believers can take comfort right now in the fact that they will avoid God's wrath against evil because of Christ. And we can trust God that He will deal with sin and evil. They will not last forever.

We Have Hope

Imagine what life was like for those first-century Christians who were confronted with threats and persecution. We may not face that kind of harassment, but in many parts of our twenty-first-century world, people do. How do Christians overcome these obstacles? How do you deal with your own pain and grief? The answer is *hope*. Regardless of our present troubles, we can look ahead with hope to a time when all who trust God will live in absolute peace. The message of Revelation must have been a great source of comfort to the believers in the first century, and it offers just as much hope to us today.

He who is the faithful witness to all these things says, "Yes, I am coming soon!" Amen! Come, Lord Jesus! (Revelation 22:20).

$\mathcal{S}$tudy the $\mathcal{W}$ord

1. What is the value of symbolic literature? Why do you think God didn't make some details of end-time events clearer for us?

2. We gave examples of an essential truth and a non-essential truth. Make a list of three additional truths in each category.

3. Read 2 Peter 3:8-14. What does this tell you about the date of Christ's return? What is the value of living a pure and blameless life before God?

4. Does the sovereignty of God comfort you or make you uneasy? Explain your answer.

   If God is sovereign, why do world events often seem out of control?

   How would you answer someone who questions the power and goodness of God in light of current conditions?

5. Jesus came to earth 2000 years ago, and He is returning to earth in the future. What is Jesus doing in the meantime? Use Scripture to support your answer.

6. Read these two statements. Then, write a paragraph about each statement, using Scripture to support each one.

    • If you are a Christian, you will persevere to the end.

    • If you persevere to the end, you are a Christian.

7. What right does God have to judge sin and sinners? Do you think God is fair in letting people who have rejected Christ face eternal punishment?

Chapter 3

The Bible ends with a flourish: vision and
song, doom and deliverance, terror and
triumph. The rush of color and sound,
image and energy, leaves us reeling. But if
we persist through the initial confusion and
read on, we begin to pick up the rhythms,
realize the connections, and find
ourselves enlisted as participants in a
multidimensional act of Christian worship.

—*Eugene Peterson in* The Message

We're ready to begin studying Revelation chapter by chapter. Now is a good time to give you a macro view of this exciting and complicated book. We're going to divide the next eleven chapters of our study into three sections:

What God Expects of Us Now (Revelation 1–3)

In chapters 3–5 we'll cover Revelation 1–3, where the glorified Christ tells John to write down "the things that are happening now" for the seven churches.

What We Can Expect in the Future (Revelation 4–18)

In chapters 5–10 we will explain (as best we can) Revelation 6–18, which talks about "the things that will happen later." Here we see John's extended vision of the coming of God's judgment against sinful humanity and the evil spiritual powers that have opposed God since Satan fell from heaven.

Our Eternal Home in Heaven (Revelation 19–22)

In chapters 11–13 we will discuss Revelation 19–22, which portrays the Second Coming of Christ followed by a thousand-year time of peace on earth, Satan's final defeat, and the time of final judgment known as the Great White Throne. Our study closes where Revelation and the Bible close—with a glorious view of heaven.

A Worship Service
for the Ages

Revelation 1:1-8

*M*ost people dig into their study of Revelation by sitting down at a desk or table with a Bible, a notepad, a stack of thick commentaries, a set of laminated end-times charts, and the latest prophecy tapes from popular Bible teachers scattered all around. As they pour through the many volumes of information and scholarly opinions, their goal is to make sense out of the 22 chapters of Revelation so they will have a better understanding of future events.

Nothing is wrong with approaching Revelation that way. But before you dive into the details, may we suggest that you look at this powerful book in an entirely new way?

Imagine yourself sitting in a worship service with a thousand other people as an eloquent speaker stands before the congregation and reads the entire book of Revelation in one sitting. Don't get nervous—it takes less than an hour. In fact, time seems to be suspended as the worship leader takes you on an incredible journey from here to eternity. As he reads the Word of God aloud, you and your fellow worshipers are transported into the very presence of God, where you bow before Him. Then, as the worship leader reads words of encouragement and rebuke, you suddenly feel ashamed and realize that you need to ask God's forgiveness for your complacency. Next, the inspired words of the apostle John take you across the vast panorama of heaven and earth as you see visions of judgment represented by the opening of seals, the sounding of trumpets, and the pouring of bowls.

Finally, you hear the dramatic story of Christ's victorious return as He tramples His enemies and rewards the faithful. The reader, now soaked in sweat from the drama of the text and the emotion of his interpretation, concludes the message of Revelation with the promise of Christ's future return.

"Yes, I am coming soon!" says the Lord.

"Amen! Come, Lord Jesus!" the entire congregation replies with one voice.

"The grace of the Lord Jesus be with you all," concludes the worship leader.

A Likely Scenario

This scenario isn't as far-fetched as you might think. The apostle John probably intended the book of Revelation to be read in the church. You see, even though he was living in exile on the island of Patmos, John was still involved with the churches on the mainland. He was still instructing and encouraging them through his writing, just as Paul did when he sent letters to the various churches from prison. Of course, John had never written anything like Revelation before, and you can be sure the churches had never heard anything like it. That's still true for us today.

If you picture Revelation as one continuous narrative rather than a series of disjointed prophetic elements, it will immediately make more sense to you, and you will ultimately get more out of it. We're not saying that studying the nuts and bolts of Revelation is pointless. If you dig deeper into the mine, you will discover some gems of unimaginable brilliance. But unless you capture the overall scope and sequence of John's "worship service," you won't know how those gems fit together to form one incredible setting. Let's see how the various elements in the first chapter of Revelation fit together.

$\mathcal{T}$he $\mathcal{M}$eaning of $\mathcal{R}$evelation

The title *Revelation* comes from the first verse in the book: "This is a revelation from Jesus Christ" (some translations say "of" Jesus Christ). Literally, *revelation* means the *uncovering* or the *unveiling* of Jesus Christ.

The Key Players (Revelation 1:1)

All Scripture is inspired by God through the Holy Spirit (2 Timothy 3:16; 2 Peter 1:20-21). John did not come up with the revelation himself. He was merely the human instrument communicating what he heard and saw. Other key players listed in 1:1 are...

Jesus Christ—The content of the message comes from the Son of God, but even He is not the author. Jesus is the *Mediator,* which is a role He has filled from the beginning. Jesus is the "one Mediator who can reconcile God and people" (1 Timothy 2:5); and He is "the one who mediates the new covenant between God and people, so that all who are invited can receive the eternal inheritance God has promised them" (Hebrews 9:15).

God—The author of Revelation and all Scripture is God the Father, who gives us all things. "Whatever is good and perfect comes to us from God above, who created all heaven's lights" (James 1:17).

An Angel—Angels are God's messengers. They announced the first coming of Jesus Christ to earth, and they are very involved in delivering the message of Revelation to John.

Touched by Angels

Thanks to popular portrayals, people tend to think of angels in one of two ways. Either they take clues from the classical paintings that show angels as cute little bare-bottomed baby cherubs, or they think angels walk among us looking like the characters in *Touched by an Angel.* While these depictions may make us feel good, the Bible paints a different and more awesome picture. Angels are God's servants who carry out some of His plans on the earth. They bring God's messages to people (Luke 1:11-19), carry out some of His judgments (Acts 12:23), battle demonic forces (Daniel 10:13), protect God's people (Psalm 91:11-12), and generally patrol the earth (Zechariah 1:10-11). In Revelation, angels are significant in the revelation of God's Word (1:1), the worship of God (5:11-12), and the execution of judgments (16:1). Angels are mentioned 67 times in Revelation.

And there are more than enough angels to go around. John writes that he saw "thousands and millions of angels" (5:11). What an amazing sight that will be when we get to heaven!

God's Other Servants—All of God's people are known in Revelation as servants. In fact, throughout the New Testament, *servant* is a title of honor, describing those who are representatives of Jesus. Your greatest calling is to serve Jesus Christ.

A Letter with Authority (1:4-6)

As we said, Revelation was written to the churches. More specifically, it was written to seven churches scattered throughout Asia Minor (we'll get to them in chapter 5). Although the number of churches is symbolic (signifying completeness), the churches aren't. These were actual churches, chosen because they were representatives of the patterns of obedience and disobedience present in the church at the end of the first century. They also represent all churches throughout the ages, including the church you attend.

The Trinity Sends Greetings

To add a little weight to his greeting, John invokes each member of the Trinity:

God the Father—He is "the one who is, who always was, and who is still to come." God is the eternal one "without beginning or end" (Psalm 90:2). Time does not apply to God. He sees the entire scope of history all at once.

God the Holy Spirit—Here the term "sevenfold Spirit" is used to describe the Holy Spirit, referring to His fullness and completeness.

God the Son—Jesus Christ is described in three powerful ways. He is...

- *The faithful witness to these things.* The word "martyr" comes from the Greek word for "witness." Jesus was sent to earth to be a martyr for our sins.

- *The first to rise from the dead.* The resurrection of Jesus from the dead is our hope that we will also be raised.

- *The commander of all the rulers of the world.* Jesus is our commander in chief, and He will be victorious in battle. We can take comfort in knowing that He will defeat not only all earthly rulers but also the spiritual rulers: Satan, sin, and death.

*T*ime and *G*od

What do you think John means when he writes in the first verse of his book that this revelation concerns the events "that will happen soon"? What do you think that phrase meant to the first-century Christians? The truth is that it means the same to us now as it did to believers 1900 years ago. Because God is not bound by time, we shouldn't think that His plan for Christ's return is on some sort of timetable. We shouldn't worry that it's been delayed. From God's perspective, the Second Coming will happen soon (remember, a thousand years is like a day to God—2 Peter 3:8). From our perspective, it could happen at any time.

Theologians use the word *imminent* to describe the future events as described in the Bible. What it means is that whether you are living in A.D. 95 or 1995, the future is always viewed as coming very soon without the necessity of an intervening time. Rather than trying to figure out the timing of the Second Coming, we need to be ready all the time, for Jesus will come back when least expected (Matthew 24:44).

The Second Coming of Jesus (1:7-8)

After reflecting on the three qualities of Jesus, John erupts in a statement of praise for the one who "freed us from our sins by shedding his blood for us" (1:5). John tells us: "Give to him everlasting glory!" (1:6). How often do you think about the awesome things Jesus has done for you? How often do you erupt in praise to Jesus and give Him the glory He deserves? If praising Jesus and giving Him glory don't come naturally, reflect on what Jesus has done for you in the past, what He's doing for you now, and what He is going to do in the future.

Speaking of the future, John now focuses on the drama of the Second Coming of Jesus, giving three descriptions of what that incredible event will be like.

Jesus will come with the clouds of heaven. Have you ever been awestruck by the powerful advance of a thunderstorm? Multiply that power by a million and imagine Jesus coming to earth with the clouds of heaven!

Everyone will see Him. Every eye will witness the return of Christ. Don't try to explain this in natural terms because it will be a supernatural event. And those who are alive will not be the only ones who see Jesus return to earth. "Even those who pierced him"—those responsible for His death on the cross—will witness this amazing event.

And all the nations of the earth will weep. The Second Coming will be, as C.S. Lewis wrote, "so beautiful to some of us and so terrible to others." Believers will weep for joy when this day comes, but everyone else will weep because they will realize that Christ is coming in judgment.

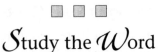

$\mathcal{S}$tudy the $\mathcal{W}$ord

1. The message of the book of Revelation took a route through these players: God→Jesus→Angel→John→Servants. Use Scripture to prove whether this is unique to Revelation or typical for the usual revelation of God's Word.

2. Why do we need a mediator between God and us? Why doesn't God deal directly with us instead of going through Jesus? Read Galatians 3:19-23 before writing down your answer.

3. Everybody seems interested in angels. Describe how you could turn a discussion with a non-Christian about angels into a discussion about Jesus.

4. Think about this statement: "The future is always viewed as coming very soon without the necessity of an intervening time." What does it mean?

   Explain this statement: God lives in the "eternal present." See John 8:58.

   What effect does this have on the way God relates to us and cares for us?

5. Each member of the Trinity is involved in the unfolding of end time events. Why is this significant?

   Use Scripture to show that the Trinity has always existed.

6. What has Jesus done for you in the past?

    What is Jesus doing for you now?

    What will Jesus do for you in the future?

7. How will everyone in the world be able to see the Second Coming at the same time? Feel free to use your imagination.

*C*hapter 4

Revelation may not satisfy our curiosity
concerning Jesus' outward appearance,
but it provides all the hope and
encouragement we could ask for with its
eloquent symbols letting us feel and
connect with who he really is.

—*Kendell H. Easley*

Wouldn't you love to know what Jesus looked like when He walked the earth? No doubt you've seen portraits of Jesus painted by people who imagined Him as a fair-haired and fair-skinned man with a serious expression on His soft and gentle face (they seem to forget that Jesus was a Jewish carpenter who spent most of His time outdoors). You can't really go by those for accuracy, so at this point you have to use your own imagination and picture Jesus in a way that is most meaningful to you.

Of course, you don't have to limit yourself to the physical characteristics of Jesus. In fact, we would suggest that you consider the vision of Jesus as described by John. Using incredible symbols that vividly portray His spiritual characteristics, John will lift your imagination and your appreciation for Jesus to new heights.

A Vision of Jesus

Revelation 1:9-20

*D*o you enjoy worshiping God? John was into it big-time, even in exile. Even though he was all alone in a "God forsaken" place, John was worshiping on the "Lord's Day." The Lord's Day was the day Christians in the first century met to worship the Lord (Acts 20:7; 1 Corinthians 16:2). John felt connected to his Christian brothers and sisters in the seven churches, and he felt connected to Jesus, so he honored the Lord on His day by worshiping Him. This theme of worship is present throughout Revelation, particularly as the saints in heaven worship the Lamb that was slain (4:10; 5:14; 7:1; 11:16; 19:4).

John is worshiping "in the Spirit." Each time this phrase occurs—here in 1:10 and again in 4:2; 17:3; and 21:10—John sees a new vision. On one level, "in the

Spirit" means that the Spirit of God inspired John's visions. But on another level—one more applicable to us—being "in the Spirit" for John meant he was worshiping God "in spirit and in truth" (John 4:24).

A Vision of Jesus (Revelation 1:9-16)

As John is worshiping the Lord, he suddenly hears a loud voice behind him "that sounded like a trumpet blast" (1:10). This is the same sound that the whole world will hear when Jesus returns to earth in the Second Coming. Jesus called it a "trumpet blast" (Matthew 24:31), and Paul called it a "trumpet sound" (1 Corinthians 15:52) and "the trumpet call of God" (1 Thessalonians 4:16). Will Jesus be the one sounding the trumpet blast with His voice when He comes again in all His glory? That seems likely.

The voice tells John to "write down what you see, and send it to the seven churches." John turns around to see the person responsible for this heavenly blast, and there standing before him is Jesus Christ. John is about to receive his first vision, and it's huge. Ever the observant one, John notices and records several characteristics of Jesus, the "Son of Man."

The Son of Man

The title "Son of Man" may not sound very lofty, but it was the title Jesus used most often to describe Himself. It refers to the heavenly Messiah, who is also human. Craig Keener writes: "The same Jesus that once lived and walked in Galilee is now described as glorious and powerful beyond imagination."

He is standing in the middle of the lampstands. Craig Keener points out that throughout the ancient world, the seven-branched lampstand, or menorah, was the most common symbol of Israel and Judaism. The seven lampstands refer to the seven churches. The image here is of Jesus standing among the churches. Even though five of the seven churches have serious problems, Jesus has not abandoned them. Jesus is faithful to the church, and as Keener writes, "it remains the place where Christ's presence is found."

He is wearing a long robe with a gold sash across His chest. The priests in the Old Testament wore long robes with golden sashes, signifying wisdom, power, and authority. The robe and sash also represent Christ as the High Priest to the churches. The function of the high priest is "to represent other human beings in their dealings with God" (Hebrews 5:1). As our High Priest, Jesus represents us before the Father (Hebrews 7:24-25).

His head and His hair are white like wool, as white as snow. The prophet Daniel wrote of the Ancient One with hair like the whitest wool (Daniel 7:9). The white hair of Jesus indicates His deity and wisdom. Because He is God, Jesus is *omniscient*. That means He knows everything. He always knows what is best for His people.

His eyes are bright like flames of fire. In another reference to Daniel (10:6), the flaming eyes of Christ symbolize His judgment of evil. It may also mean that Jesus sees everything, which means He is *omnipresent*. That is, He is everywhere at once.

His feet are as bright as bronze refined in a furnace. Glowing metal always signifies power. Bronze was the source of Roman military strength (the army used bronze shields and breastplates). Here the image is of Christ stomping out evil and those who have been unfaithful to

Him. The imagery suggests that Christ is *omnipotent*. That means He is all-powerful.

His voice thunders like mighty ocean waves. If you have ever stood near the ocean as it pounded on the shore, you know the power of crashing water—and it never stops. Christ speaks with supreme power and authority, and His Word goes on forever. Like the constant pounding of the waves, which never stop, the voice of Jesus is relentless.

He holds seven stars in His right hand. The right hand signifies the place of power. Later Jesus identifies the seven stars as the angels of the seven churches. As we will soon discover, the seven angels are those who receive the seven letters. The fact that Jesus has them in His hand tells us that He is never going to let them go.

A sharp two-edged sword comes from His mouth. The Romans invented the double-edged sword and used it to conquer many armies. The sword coming from the mouth of Jesus indicates precise power and force. In Hebrews the Word of God is described as sharper than a two-edged sword (Hebrews 4:12 KJV). The Word of Christ is the Word of God.

His face is as bright as the sun in all its brilliance. This describes Christ in all His glory and majesty. It also symbolizes His deity.

The Power of Jesus (1:17-20)

As you can imagine, this awesome image of the glorified Christ caused John to fall to the feet of Jesus. This wasn't the first time John saw Jesus in this way. Years earlier Jesus was transfigured while Peter, James, and John watched (Matthew 17:1-8). They fell at the feet of Jesus as well. Jesus tells John now what He told the three disciples then:

"Don't be afraid!" He then tells John why He is worthy of glory and honor (and fear).

Have You Seen Jesus, My Lord?

After John saw this incredible picture of Jesus, he fell at the feet of Jesus "as dead" (1:17). Jesus then placed His right hand on John and said, "Don't be afraid!" He was blessing John and reassuring him. How about you? Have you been blessed by Jesus because you have worshiped Him for who He really is? What is your picture of Jesus? Do you see Him as the quiet man from Galilee who walked the dusty trails like a vagabond, loving and healing people out of love and compassion? Do you picture Him like those old paintings of a soft and silky Jesus? Or do you see Jesus as John saw Him—the mighty warrior and conquering king who rules the universe with power and glory and honor? We know the human Jesus, but too often we neglect the Jesus that John saw that day on Patmos. If we could see Jesus for who He is, our lives would be changed. Pray and ask Jesus to show Himself to you in a way that will knock you to your knees and change your life.

He is God (1:17). Earlier God said, "I am the Alpha and the Omega" (1:8). Jesus equates Himself with God when He says, "I am the First and the Last." Because He is God, Jesus has always existed. Paul writes: "He existed before everything else began, and he holds all creation together" (Colossians 1:17).

He is alive (1:18). The whole Good News message of Jesus hinges on the resurrection (1 Corinthians 15:16-19). Jesus confirms that He is the Resurrected One when He says, "I am the living one who died." This echoes the words of Jesus as recorded by John in his Gospel:

> *I am the resurrection and the life. Those who believe in me, even though they die like everyone else, will*

live again. They are given eternal life for believing in me and will never perish (John 11:25-26).

He has power over sin (1:18). When Jesus says, "I am alive forever and ever!" He is saying that He has conquered sin forever.

He has power over death (1:18). Sin resulted in death for the entire human race, so when Jesus conquered sin, He also defeated death. When Jesus says, "I hold the keys of death and the grave," He demonstrates that He hasn't just conquered death—He controls it as well. Jesus alone can determine who will die and who won't.

Write This Down

Put yourself in John's sandals for a moment. You've just heard the trumpet blast of the voice of Jesus, you've seen a brilliant vision of Jesus, and Jesus has just told you how powerful He is. Do you think your eyes and your mouth would be as wide as they could be? Would your hands be trembling? Absolutely. Yet you wouldn't miss the signal that Jesus had a message He wanted delivered to the people then and to people now.

Jesus has chosen John to be a witness to "the things that are now happening and the things that will happen later" (1:19). Jesus is in charge of all of history—past, present, and future. As His people, we can take comfort in that, no matter how out of control things seem to get. Jesus—and Jesus alone—is in control.

Recurring Themes, Images, and Numbers

In this chapter we've seen the images of "in the Spirit," the seven churches, and trumpets. These are just a few of the many recurring symbols that are going to pop up from here on. Merrill Tenney points out several interesting sets of themes and images that provide clues to the content of Revelation.

In the Spirit—Four visions are introduced by the phrase "in the Spirit" (1:10; 4:2; 17:1-3; 21:9-10).

Seven—Several series of sevens appear throughout Revelation. The number *seven* is very important throughout Scripture. McGee writes that it signifies completeness. Revelation includes...

- seven churches (2:1,8,12,18; 3:1,7,14)

- seven spirits of God (4:5)

- seven seals (6:1,3,5,7,9,12; 8:1)

- seven trumpets (8:6-8,10,12; 9:1,13; 11:15)

- seven thunders (10:3)

- seven bowls (16:1-4,8,10,12,17)

- seven major personages (12:1,3,5,7; 13:1,11; 14:1)

- seven blessings (1:3; 14:13; 16:15; 19:9; 20:6; 22:7,14)

Other numbers—Several other combinations of numbers pop up throughout the book: 24 elders (4:4), 4 living creatures (4:6), 4 horsemen (6:1-8), 4 angels (9:14), 144,000 of the redeemed (7:4; 14:1), 12 gates in the walls of the holy city guarded by 12 angels (21:12), 12 foundation stones (21:14), and 12 kinds of fruit in the tree of life (22:2).

Study the Word

1. What does worshiping God "in spirit and in truth" mean?

   Describe your most meaningful worship experience.

   What kind of blessing did you receive afterward?

2. Reflect on the trumpet blast of 1:10. Have you ever thought that the trumpet sound described by Paul in 1 Corinthians 15:52 could be made by Jesus? What will be the effect of this mighty sound?

3. Reflect on the nine dramatic characteristics of Jesus recorded by John in 1:12-16. Describe how each one impacts you personally:

    • He is standing in the middle of the lampstands.

    • He is wearing a long robe with a gold sash across His chest.

    • His head and His hair are white like wool, as white as snow.

    • His eyes are bright like flames of fire.

    • His feet are as bright as bronze refined in a furnace.

    • His voice thunders like mighty ocean waves.

    • He holds the seven stars in His right hand.

    • A sharp two-edged sword comes from His mouth.

    • His face is as bright as the sun in all its brilliance.

4. In 1:17-18 Jesus makes four statements about Himself. Why must each of these statements be absolutely true in order for Jesus to be our Savior and Lord?

    • I am the First and the Last.

    • I am the living one who died.

    • I am alive forever and ever!

    • I hold the keys of death and the grave.

5. Of the four major visions in Revelation, the first one is of Jesus. What is the significance of this?

Chapter 5

I'm not asking you to take them out of the
world, but to keep them safe from the evil
one. They are not part of this world any
more than I am. Make them pure and holy
by teaching them your words of truth.

—*Jesus Christ*
JOHN 17:15-17

We're just as anxious as you are to dig into the details of the seals, the trumpets, and the bowls of judgment that make Revelation unique. We can't wait to discuss the Great Tribulation, the Second Coming, the Great White Throne, and heaven with you. But we're not quite there yet. Before we look at "the things that will happen later," we have to consider "the things that are now happening" (1:19).

These are the things that Jesus needed to tell the seven churches in first-century Asia. Located in the western part of present-day Turkey, these were actual historical churches. The seven churches are long since gone, but the messages they received are completely applicable to those of us living in the twenty-first century. So get ready for a contemporary message drawn from an ancient book.

Letters to the Seven Churches

Revelation 2–3

*A*s soon as John recovers from his encounter with the living Christ, he has a job to do. Jesus dictates a series of seven letters—messages, really—to the seven churches. John is to write down "the things that are now happening" (1:19). He probably has some basic knowledge of what's going on in these churches, but Jesus knows everything. Jesus has divine knowledge. He knows what's going on inside the hearts of the believers in these churches.

Jesus loves the church because it's His body, active and alive on earth. Even though He dictated these letters to historic churches a little over 1900 years ago, the messages are timeless. The things that pleased Jesus then still please Him today. And the things that caused Him to complain then cause Him grief today. So as you read what Jesus has to say to the seven churches in Revelation, apply His words to you and your church.

Although each message is different, each one follows a similar pattern. First, Jesus gives a *characteristic* about Himself. He then *compliments* the church before issuing His *complaint*. Finally, Jesus offers a *correction* for each church. If they do what He says, He makes a *commitment* to honor their obedience.

*W*ho *W*ere the *A*ngels?

Each of the seven letters is written to "an angel of the church." This refers to the pastor of each church. In addition to receiving the letter addressed to his church, each pastor also received the letters to the other six churches because each church got the entire book of Revelation.

Ephesus: Return to Your First Love (Revelation 2:1-7)

Ephesus was a major center of commerce and tourism in the Roman Empire. The great temple of Artemis, one of the seven wonders of the ancient world, was there. The Ephesian church was the leading one in the area.

Characteristic: Jesus says He is the one holding the seven stars in His right hand and is walking among the seven gold lampstands, signifying His personal involvement in the church. He knew the Ephesian church—and all the churches, for that matter—intimately.

Compliment: Jesus commends the Ephesians for their hard work, their patient endurance, and their discernment of evil and false teaching.

Complaint: Despite their diligence and doctrinal discernment, the Ephesians have fallen from their first love. Even though they are biblically literate, they have lost their love for Christ and for each other.

Correction: Jesus asks them to remember their first love and to turn back to Him again. If they don't, He will remove their influence. (Historical note: Ephesus declined as a major city from this point forward, and the area has been uninhabited since the fourteenth century.)

Commitment: If they do what Jesus asks, Jesus promises that they will "eat from the tree of life in the paradise of God." The tree of life was in the Garden of Eden, so this imagery signifies eternal life.

Smyrna: Don't Be Afraid of What You Are About to Suffer (Revelation 2:8-11)

Smyrna was a large and wealthy seaport city about 35 miles north of Ephesus.

Characteristic: Jesus calls Himself "the First and the Last, who died and is alive." He is identifying with those who are physically suffering yet spiritually alive.

Compliment: Jesus assures the Christians in Smyrna that even though they are poor in this world, they have won true riches.

Complaint: Jesus has no complaint against these suffering Christians.

Correction: No complaint, no correction. Instead, Jesus tells them they will have more persecution and more suffering. He even gives the details.

Commitment: If the church at Smyrna can hang in there and remain faithful to Jesus in the face of persecution and even death, they will receive the "crown of life." In the end, God will vindicate them. This is a promise for all persecuted and suffering Christians in all ages. (Historical note: Today Smyrna is a large seaport with a population of 200,000.)

Pergamum: Repent (Revelation 2:12-17)

Located about 20 miles inland from Smyrna, Pergamum was a wealthy but wicked city.

Characteristic: Jesus makes reference to His two-edged sword, implying that He is about to expose these believers for who they really are (Hebrews 4:12).

Compliment: Although the believers at Pergamum lived among a stronghold of Satan, they refused to deny Christ and remained loyal to Him.

Complaint: Despite its loyalty, the church was tolerating some false teachers who taught pagan doctrine and immorality. The bottom line is that adultery was common in the church.

Correction: In a word, Jesus tells them to repent or else! Unless they turn from their wicked ways, Jesus will bring judgment against them. Things haven't changed in our churches today. Christians think they can get away with an immoral lifestyle. They think they can hide it from God, but life doesn't work that way. Jesus knows all and sees all. We often think judgment won't come in this life, especially to believers, but it will. God will not tolerate compromise with the culture and with sin indefinitely.

Commitment: Jesus promises that anyone who repents will eat "hidden manna" and receive a "white stone" with a new name. Both of these are symbols for eternal life.

Thyatira: Hold Tightly to What You Have (Revelation 2:18-29)

This smaller city was 40 miles southeast of Pergamum. The church here was small as well, but it had some big problems.

Characteristic: Jesus characterizes Himself with flaming eyes and polished bronze feet. His bright eyes symbolize complete knowledge, and his bronze feet represent power.

Compliment: Unlike the Ephesians, these Christians demonstrated love, and they were making improvements in this area.

Complaint: They may have excelled in their brotherly love, but they didn't know the Scriptures. There was a "Jezebel" in their midst who was deceiving them, and they were being taken in. The original Jezebel was a wicked Old Testament queen who encouraged the worship of the pagan deity Baal. The Jezebel in the church at Thyatira is someone posing as a prophet. Jesus is really ticked off at this woman, who is deliberately leading Christians into sexual immorality and pagan worship. Worse, some believers are following her teachings, calling them "deep truths." That's a bunch of baloney, says Jesus (or words to that effect). These "deep truths" are in fact the "depths of Satan."

Correction: Jesus offers the severest possible rebuke. Unless the believers turn away from their evil deeds and hold tight to the truth they have been taught, He will give them what they deserve (and that can't be good). Jesus goes so far as to guarantee that unrepentant believers will suffer and some will even die.

Commitment: Jesus promises that those who overcome this threat of false teaching will share in His authority over the nations.

$\mathcal{T}$ake $\mathcal{C}$harge of $\mathcal{Y}$our $\mathcal{S}$piritual $\mathcal{L}$ife

We have to take responsibility for our knowledge of God's Word. We have no excuse for falling prey to ideas that run contrary to the truth about God. We need to regularly search the Scriptures because Jesus "searches out the thoughts and intentions of every person."

Sardis: Wake Up! (Revelation 3:1-6)

Sardis was another wealthy city, located 30 miles southeast of Thyatira.

Characteristic: As before, Jesus is holding the seven stars, and He also has "the sevenfold spirit." This shows His relationship to the Holy Spirit.

Compliment: Jesus gives the church a backhanded compliment: "You have a reputation for being alive—but you are dead." They were hypocrites, appearing on the outside to be spiritual, but on the inside they were spiritually dead.

Complaint: Their deeds were "far from right in the sight of God." They weren't engaging in heresy or immorality like the believers at Pergamum and Thyatira, but they were faking their spirituality, and that hypocrisy offended Jesus.

Correction: Jesus offers a three-step plan to help them "wake up" spiritually: Go back to what you heard and believed at first, hold to it firmly, and turn to Jesus again.

Commitment: If you remain faithful in your daily walk with Christ, you are going to find your name written in the Book of Life. This is what Peter meant when he wrote:

> *So, dear brothers and sisters, work hard to prove that you really are among those God has called and chosen. Doing this, you will never stumble or fall away. And God will open wide the gates of heaven for you to enter into the eternal Kingdom of our Lord and Savior Jesus Christ* (2 Peter 1:10-11).

This was true for the church in Sardis, and it's true for you.

Get Back to Basics

We all need the kind of advice Jesus gave to the church at Sardis. Perhaps you have been exposed to solid, accurate Bible teaching but have strayed from what you know. You're keeping up a good front, but your spiritual life is in retreat. You need to go back to the basics. Rediscover the joy of Bible study, prayer, fellowship, and worship. Then stay in the Word and walk closely with the Lord. Whatever direction you were going, turn around and turn to Jesus. Return to your first love.

Philadelphia: Hold On to What You Have (Revelation 3:7-13)

Yes, this was the city of brotherly love, but this one was located 25 miles southeast of Sardis. (Historical note: Believers have lived here to this day.)

Characteristic: Here Jesus describes Himself as having the key of David. This refers to Christ the Messiah, who alone decides who will live in His kingdom and who will not.

Compliment: Jesus has no complaint or correction, only this commendation: "I know all the things you do, and I have opened a door that no one can shut." This is the open door to heaven, and Jesus has the key. Jesus also commends the Philadelphians for obeying His Word even when they had "little strength." The believers have been experiencing persecution from the Jews.

Commitment: Impressed with their perseverance, Jesus promises to protect them from "the great time of testing" that is coming. Scholars generally agree this refers to the Great Tribulation, although they disagree on what Jesus means when He says, "I will protect you." Those words could be interpreted to mean that the believers will be taken out of the world before the time of testing begins. Or they could mean that God will protect believers during the Great Tribulation. We'll discuss this more in the next chapter.

Laodicea: Be Diligent and Turn from Your Indifference (Revelation 3:14-22)

Laodicea was another wealthy city, located 40 miles southeast of Philadelphia on the road to Colosse.

Characteristic: Jesus identifies Himself as the God of truth who is completely trustworthy.

Complaint: Jésus has nothing good to say about the Laodiceans. Instead, He gives them one of the most scathing judgments in all of Scripture.

I know the things you do, that you are neither hot nor cold. I wish you were one or the other! But since you are like lukewarm water, I will spit you out of my mouth! (Revelation 3:15-16).

Hot and Cold Water

People generally think that Jesus prefers someone who is cold to God rather than someone who is lukewarm. This isn't what this means at all. The simple matter is that Laodicea had a lousy, lukewarm water supply, unlike two nearby cities. To the northwest, Hierapolis was well known for its hot, therapeutic mineral springs. To the southeast was Colosse, where the water was cold and refreshing. Both hot and cold water have value, but lukewarm water is useless, especially when it's filled with impurities, as was the water of Laodicea. Jesus was unhappy with the Laodiceans because the effect of their lives was neither therapeutic nor refreshing. They were as useless as their water. They had become complacent and self-satisfied. God hates to see believers get this way. The meaning of "spit you out of my mouth" is closer to vomiting than spitting. Jesus rejects indifferent, self-satisfied, lukewarm believers in the worst way. He calls them "wretched and miserable and poor and blind and naked."

Correction: The cure for spiritual indifference is to look to the Lord rather than depending on yourself. Laodicea was a banking center. The people had plenty of money, but they needed to buy gold refined by fire. They were known for producing garments made from black wool, but what they needed was pure white clothing.

Laodicea had a medical school where people could buy a special ointment to soothe their eyes. What these spiritually lukewarm Christians needed was spiritual sight.

Commitment: Jesus paints one of the most vivid and inviting pictures in the entire Bible. It stands as an encouragement to all who need the healing touch and eternal salvation only Christ can offer.

> *Look! Here I stand at the door and knock. If you hear me calling and open the door, I will come in, and we will share a meal as friends* (Revelation 3:20).

Jesus closes this section to the churches with an appeal to anyone who will hear Him and His message. People today would do well to listen to the Lord.

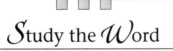

Study the Word

1. What are the common threads that run through the letters to the seven churches?

How many apply to churches today?

Reflect on your own church for a moment. Which complaints against the seven churches seem to hit closest to home?

2. Can you remember the first time you first fell in love with Jesus? What was that like?

Describe the attitudes and actions of someone who is in love with Jesus.

Now describe the actions and attitudes of a Christian who has fallen out of love with Jesus.

3. Jesus promises the crown of life to those who remain faithful even when facing death. For more on the crown of life and the eternal prize, read 1 Corinthians 9:25; 2 Timothy 2:5; James 1:12; and 1 Peter 5:4.

In what ways do these verses motivate you to live for Christ now?

What significance will the crown of life have in eternity?

4. Can you think of any modern-day "Jezebels" who are leading Christians astray? What is the best defense against false prophets? See 2 Timothy 3:1-9.

5. Christians are often accused of being hypocritical. Do you think this is a legitimate criticism?

    What is the antidote for spiritual hypocrisy?

6. Why do you think Jesus is so repulsed by lukewarm Christians?

    We all go through seasons of lukewarm behavior. What are the biggest disadvantages to staying in this "no-man's-land"?

7. Read Revelation 3:20-22. Do the words of Jesus apply only to the "lost," or could they apply to Christians as well? Explain.

Chapter 6

Revelation is filled with encouragement.
It is a book that will either inspire your
faith—or it will fill you with fear. It will give
you great comfort and encouragement if you
know the Lord of all time and all space.
But it is also a solemn book designed to
make us understand that the One who
unrolls the scroll is the One who was once
here, the One who died on Calvary's cross,
the Lamb led to slaughter so that He
might win the right to be the Lion,
the King of all the earth.

—*Ray Stedman*

The first vision of John is now complete. The next vision begins in Revelation 4 with an incredible sight. In fact, it is the most amazing sight anyone could ever see. John sees "a door standing open in heaven." Then the trumpet-blast voice of Jesus tells John, "Come up here, and I will show you what must happen after these things." Talk about an invitation you wouldn't want to refuse! The scene of Revelation now shifts as John is transported from earth to heaven "in the Spirit."

The next five chapters in this study are going to cover the visions John sees in heaven. Here is where we find the incredible (and sometimes confusing) images and symbols Revelation is famous for. Just so you know where we are going, here is an outline of what we're going to cover in chapters 6 through 10:

- chapter 6: God and the Lamb (Revelation 4–5)
- chapter 7: The Seven Seals (Revelation 6–7)
- chapter 8: The Seven Trumpets (Revelation 8–11)
- chapter 9: An Epic Drama for the Ages (Revelation 12–14)
- chapter 10: The Seven Bowls and the Great Prostitute (Revelation 15–18)

God and the Lamb

Revelation 4–5

Revelation 4 and 5 describe John's vision of the throne of God in heaven. They show us that God is the ruler of the universe. Thrones always represent the power and sovereignty of the one who sits there. If you lived in a kingdom with a king sitting on the throne, you would know that nothing happened unless the king said so. Well, you do live in a kingdom—God's kingdom. And nothing happens now and nothing will happen in the future that is outside of God's control and command. No matter what happens on earth, God in heaven is in charge of it all. The first thing John sees after he is taken to heaven is the throne of God.

How Did John Get to Heaven?

So how was John transported to heaven? Was he beamed up like a character from *Star Trek,* was he snatched into the air and carried along at supersonic speed, or did his spirit go to heaven while his body stayed behind? The Bible isn't clear. The apostle Paul wrote about a similar experience of being "caught up into the third heaven." Paul can only speculate as to how he got there. "Whether my body was there or just my spirit, I don't know; only God knows. But I do know that I was caught up into paradise and heard things so astounding that they cannot be told" (2 Corinthians 12:3-4). By whatever means John got to heaven, he was there, and heaven was real. And most importantly for us, he wrote about what he saw in detail through the divine inspiration of the Holy Spirit.

The Throne of God (Revelation 4:1-3)

John describes the awesome sight of God on His throne. He doesn't describe God's features but rather His supernatural splendor. John uses brilliant gemstones to describe the majesty of the throne. According to Dr. John Walvoord, the ruby red carnelian and green jasper jewels were the first and the last of the 12 gemstones worn on the robes of the high priests (Exodus 28:17-21). God is the first and the last of all creation (Revelation 1:8). The rainbow circling God's throne indicates the eternal promises of God to the human race.

Picture the throne of God with flashes of brilliant red and green and the radiance of a rainbow. Imagine the energy of the lightning and the rumbling of the thunder emanating from the throne. John saw all this, and someday all of those in heaven will see God's mighty power!

The 24 Elders and the 4 Living Beings (Revelation 4:4-11)

John sees 24 elders on 24 thrones. Bible scholars have offered a dozen different interpretations about who or what they are. One common view is that the elders represent the 12 tribes of Israel in the Old Testament and the 12 apostles in the New Testament, symbolizing both Jews and Gentiles whom God has saved. The other view is that they are 24 angels who have been given the responsibility of surrounding God's throne.

Each of the four living beings had its own form: One was like a lion, another like an ox, the third was like a human, and the fourth was like an eagle. John wasn't literally looking at three animals and a human. He was watching four beings who were worshiping God. These same four beings are mentioned 14 times in Revelation, so they must be important. Certainly they tell us that worship is an integral part of heaven. Along with the elders, the four beings say:

> *You are worthy, O Lord our God, to receive glory and honor and power. For you created everything, and it is for your pleasure that they exist and were created* (Revelation 4:11).

Who Are the Four Living Beings?

We shouldn't get carried away with trying to read too much into the symbolism of Revelation, but sometimes various interpretations can help us appreciate God even more. A good example is the meaning of the four living beings, who seem to symbolize God and His attributes. The wings show that God is everywhere, and the eyes show that He sees all and knows all. The lion represents the majesty of God, the ox His strength, the man represents His intelligence, and the eagle shows us that God is above all.

Another view, expressed by Kendell Easley, says that each creature represents a different Gospel and therefore a different characteristic of Jesus:

- **Lion**—*Matthew*, where Jesus is the Lion of Judah, the King of the Jews

- **Ox**—*Mark*, where Jesus is the servant

- **Man**—*Luke*, which emphasizes the humanity of Jesus

- **Eagle**—*John*, which shows Jesus as the heavenly one who brings us eternal life

The Scroll (Revelation 5:1-5)

The next thing John sees is "a scroll in the right hand of the one who was sitting on the throne." This scroll is a key to the book of Revelation. In fact, as we're going to find out, the scroll contains the information that makes up the rest of the book. The contents of the scroll are revealed through the seven seals, the seven trumpets, and the seven bowls. All of these are going to show God's judgment against sin. Here's how this series of "sevens" is going to progress:

Seven seals are on the scroll. In John's day, some books and documents were written on scrolls and then sealed with clay or wax in order to keep the contents safe and secret. You couldn't read the scroll until the seal was broken. The seven seals on God's scroll (we will cover these in chapter 7) show that God has shut this scroll very tight and kept it a secret—until now.

Underneath the seventh seal are the seven trumpets. The seventh seal will be broken in Revelation 8, revealing the seven trumpet judgments (we will cover these in chapter 8). The seven trumpets will describe God's judgments at the end of the world.

The seventh trumpet will announce the seven bowls. Beginning in Revelation 15, the seven bowl judgments are poured out against sin and Satan (we'll cover this in chapter 10).

Why Is John Crying?

When John sees the scroll and realizes that no one is able to open and read it, he begins to weep. Why is John crying? John knows that unless the scroll can be opened, the final judgment of God against sin cannot begin. Without the judgment of God, sin and evil will continue unchecked, and there is no hope and no future for the people of God. We can thank God and praise Him that Someone is able and worthy to open the scroll so that God can judge evil once and for all.

Worthy Is the Lamb (Revelation 5:6-14)

One of the 24 elders tells John to stop his crying. "Look, the Lion of the tribe of Judah, the heir to David's throne, has conquered. He is worthy to open the scroll and break its seven seals." What wonderful news for John and for us! Sin and evil will be conquered.

When John turns to look at this Lion of Judah, he sees something unexpected: a Lamb. And not just any ordinary lamb. This Lamb "had been killed but was now standing between the throne and the four living beings and among the twenty-four elders." What a striking image, and John knew exactly who it was. Throughout Scripture, the lamb has represented a sacrifice to God:

- Just as Abraham was about to sacrifice his son Isaac, God provided a ram instead (Genesis 22:13-14).

- The prophet Isaiah foretold the coming Messiah, who would be "led as a lamb to the slaughter" (Isaiah 53:7).

- John the Baptist saw Jesus and said: "Look! There is the Lamb of God who takes away the sin of the world!" (John 1:29).

This Lamb in Revelation, who is worthy to open the scroll, is the Savior, who died for the sins of the world. This is the same Lamb of God who gave His life for us so that by believing in His name, we might have eternal life (John 3:16). The Lamb, of course, is Jesus.

Although Jesus is the sacrificial Lamb, He is not dead, and He is not weak. He is alive with resurrection power. His seven horns and seven eyes symbolize His perfect power and wisdom. Jesus alone is worthy to open the scroll of judgment against sin because He alone has conquered sin for all time. That's why John saw the 24 elders and the four living beings and "thousands and millions of angels around the throne" worshiping the Lamb as they sang:

The Lamb is worthy—the Lamb who was killed. He is worthy to receive power and riches and wisdom and strength and honor and glory and blessing (Revelation 5:12).

"Thousands and Millions"?

John writes that he saw thousands and millions of angels. How many is that? The Greek language did not have a word to describe the number of angelic beings John saw. More than likely, he saw too many to count. Can you envision 100 million angels? How about a billion? Even those numbers are too small!

■ ■ ■

Study the Word

1. As you read about the images of heaven, did you notice that the materials John sees in heaven are also found on earth? What do you think? Will heaven contain the same elements of beauty that we have on earth, or was this probably the only way John could describe what he saw?

2. What do you need to do to make sure God is sitting on the throne of your life?

    Can a Christian live with God in his or her life but not on the throne? For how long?

3. Reflect on the four creatures in 4:7. Find a verse or a passage in each of the four Gospels that shows a specific characteristic of Jesus:

    • Matthew (lion) —

    • Mark (ox)—

    • Luke (man)—

    • John (eagle) —

4. Most people would be delighted if they knew for sure that their sin would never be judged. Yet John cries in 5:4 because he isn't sure God is going to judge sin and evil. What should be our attitude toward sin? How do we embrace God's judgment against sin while still loving the sinner?

5. In his Gospel, the apostle John (the same John who wrote Revelation) writes that John the Baptist called Jesus "the Lamb of God." Later in his Gospel, John quotes Jesus as saying, "I am the good shepherd" (John 10:11). How can Jesus be both a sacrificial lamb and a shepherd?

6. Read John 10:11-16 and list the qualities that are common to both Jesus the Lamb and Jesus the Shepherd.

Chapter 7

The Book of Revelation has been labeled a book difficult to understand. Some folk say that it is just a mumbo jumbo of a great many visions that are out of this world and that no one can understand. It is my conviction that this book is very logical and is divided in a very simple manner that no one can miss.

—*J. Vernon McGee*

One of the big reasons most people—including many Christians—don't take Revelation seriously is that they don't think the symbolism and the meaning relate to their lives right now. For the most part, the message of Revelation seems like it belongs in another place and another time.

To some extent, that's true. Much of Revelation concerns a future time when the earth will be a much different—and a much more horrible—place than it is now. Those of us living in relative peace and prosperity struggle to believe that someday the earth is going to be the worst place imaginable because God's patience with sin and sinners is finally going to run out. But that's exactly what's going to happen. We're not trying to alarm you. What we would rather do is alert you. Revelation may seem like fiction, but nothing could be further from the truth. The events in this chapter are very, very true. And they could come at any time.

The Seven Seals

Revelation 6–7

*I*n Revelation 6 the Lamb of God begins to break the seals, thereby setting into motion the series of seal, trumpet, and bowl judgments. Alan Johnson points out that the seals parallel the signs of the approaching end times Jesus talked about in the Olivet Discourse (Matthew 24). In this "sermon" Jesus divided the events of the last days into three periods:

1. the beginning of the horror to come (Matthew 24:8)

2. a time of greater horror known as the Great Tribulation (Matthew 24:21)

3. the Second Coming of Christ (Matthew 24:29-31)

The seven seals seem to follow this pattern. The first four seals are broken to reveal judgments upon the earth prior to the last days, while the last three seals reveal cosmic disasters that characterize the Great Tribulation and lead up to the Second Coming.

The Four Horsemen (Revelation 6:1-8)

Among the most vivid and frightening images in Revelation are the four horsemen—sometimes called the Four Horsemen of the Apocalypse—who come from the first four seals. Each of the four horses is a different color and each horseman is given a different power over the earth. Together they represent God's judgment of people's sin and rebellion.

- *The first horseman* rides a *white* horse and wins many battles and gains victory. Walvoord sees the horseman as the Antichrist, the same future world ruler predicted in Daniel 9:26-27 and Revelation 13. Others see the rider representing mankind's bloody lust for power and conquest, which leads to the characteristics of the next three horsemen: warfare, famine, and death.

- *The second horseman* rides a *red* horse, symbolizing war and bloodshed.

- *The third horseman* rides a *black* horse, symbolizing poverty and famine, which are the effects of war and bloodshed.

- *The fourth horseman* rides a *pale green* horse, the color of a corpse. This horseman is called Death, the final result of warfare, famine, and disease.

The number *four* in Revelation often represents the world (as in the four corners of the earth). Some interpreters see the four horsemen as representing worldwide calamities that have occurred through the ages. Easley writes: "The four horsemen have thundered down through history and all around the globe." They will continue to unleash their dark power, but only as long as Christ permits.

Why Does Christ Permit Such Destruction?

Whether you interpret the four horsemen as representing ongoing historical calamities or a future time of great destruction, you may be wondering how Jesus can permit warfare, famine, and death. We must keep in mind that Jesus doesn't send these disasters. The lust for power and the desire to conquer and kill already exist in the heart of humanity. This is the result of sin, which we brought on ourselves when we rebelled against God. By breaking the seals, Christ demonstrates His control over history. And as Revelation unfolds, He will show His complete triumph over sin and evil. What an encouragement this must have been to the first-century Christians, who were experiencing severe persecution. This should also encourage us.

In addition, we need to see how these four horsemen represent God's mercy. They are given authority over only one-fourth of the earth (6:8). Rather than wiping out the whole earth all at once, God is still giving unbelievers time to turn to Christ.

The Martyrs Cry Out (Revelation 6:9-17)

If the four horsemen are sent by God to judge sin and evil, what will happen to the Christians during this time? How will God deal with His people during the time of judgment? If you accept the interpretation that the judgments of the four horsemen have been going on throughout history, then the following explanation makes sense.

With the opening of the fifth seal, John sees the souls of "all who had been martyred for the Word of God and for being faithful in their witness." These are all of the people who have been killed through the centuries for their faith in Christ (165,000 people were martyred in the year 2000 alone). These martyrs that John sees in heaven cry out and ask when God will avenge their death. They are told to rest a little longer until the full measure of the servants of Jesus had been martyred. In other words, the suffering is not over. More will be killed for their faith.

Then the Lamb opens the sixth seal, unleashing a series of cataclysmic events that affect the earth, the sun, the moon, the stars, and the mountains. This is the coming of the wrath of the Lamb against sin and all those who refuse to repent and turn to God. Whereas the effects of the first four seals (the four horsemen) could be going on right now, clearly the destruction of the sixth seal involves future events tied to the end of the world. Again we ask the question, What about God's people? Where are they when things really heat up and the wrath of the Lamb is unleashed? The answer comes in Revelation 7.

Sealed by God (Revelation 7)

Just as the destruction is about to begin, an angel brings "the seal of the living God." This seal is placed on the foreheads of God's people to indicate they are owned by God. By contrast, the "mark of the beast" will be placed on those who deny God to indicate they are owned by Satan (Revelation 13:16-18).

Just what does this seal of the living God do? Does it keep God's people from being harmed or killed? In a physical sense, not necessarily. But in a spiritual and eternal sense, absolutely. Even though they may face the wrath of evil people and a godless culture—which is temporary—believers will never face the wrath of God, which is eternal.

Believers and the Great Tribulation

One of the great debates about the end times concerns the Great Tribulation, which is a seven-year period when the Antichrist will rule right before Christ returns. The first half of the Tribulation will be a time of worldwide peace, followed by three-and-a-half years of incredible destruction. Here are three views on where Christians will be when the Great Tribulation occurs:

1. Christians will be raptured before the Tribulation.

This view holds that all believers, dead and alive, will be caught up in the air (or *raptured*) to be with the Lord *before* the seven-year Tribulation begins. Then, after the Tribulation, Christ will return to earth in the Second Coming to defeat Satan and his armies and establish a literal Millennium. (People who believe in a literal Millennium are called *premillennialists*. More about the Millennium in the chapter 12.) This is the *premillennial, pretribulational* view.

2. Christians will go through the first half of the Tribulation.

Some premillennialists believe that Christians will be around for the first half of the Tribulation but will be raptured before things get really messy in the second half. This is the *midtribulational* view (also known as the *prewrath Rapture* view).

3. Christians will go through the Tribulation.

Some premillennialists have concluded that Christians will remain on earth through the future seven-year Great Tribulation. In this view, the Rapture and the Second Coming happen simultaneously, followed by the defeat of Satan's armies and the Millennium. This is the *posttribulational* view.

We must not get bogged down in the "pretrib/midtrib/posttrib" debate. Nothing is wrong with asking God to remove us from the horrors of the Tribulation (Jesus suggested that in Luke 21:36), but we should be prepared for difficult times. Never forget that many people in the world are experiencing persecution right now, and many are being killed for their faith. Just because you are now free to worship God in any way you choose doesn't mean you always will be. As far as timing goes, we need to remember that the return of Christ can happen at any time, and it will come when people least expect it (Matthew 24:44). We must always be ready.

If we can disagree on the timing of the Rapture, then we can agree on this: The seal of the living God means that God will protect us no matter what happens. Read again the words of Christ to the persecuted church in Philadelphia:

> *Because you have obeyed my command to persevere, I will protect you from the great time of testing that will come upon the whole world to test those who belong to this world* (Revelation 3:10).

*W*ho *A*re the 144,000?

Some people interpret the "144,000 who were sealed from all the tribes of Israel" (7:4) as just that—144,000 people from the nation of Israel who will be saved in the last days. Other interpreters see the number 144,000 as representing completeness. The number probably symbolizes all of God's true followers, Jews and Gentiles alike. The Life Application Commentary states:

> All of God's followers will be brought safely to him; not one will be overlooked or forgotten. God seals these believers either by withdrawing them from the earth in the Rapture or by giving them special strength and courage to make it through this time of great persecution. No matter what happens, they will be brought to their reward of eternal life. Their destiny is secure.

Washed in the Blood

Christianity has sometimes been called a "bloody" religion. We tend to shy away from such a description because we tend to equate blood with injury and death. In fact, blood is the basis of all physical life. The Bible is filled with blood, and not just here in Revelation. In the Old Testament, God was very specific in saying that no person could eat or drink blood, "for the life of any creature is in its blood." God said, "It is the blood, representing life, that brings you atonement" (Leviticus 17:11).

Just as the blood of the Lamb washed the robes of those coming out of the Tribulation and made them white (Revelation 7:14), the blood of Christ washes away our sins and makes us clean before God (1 Peter 1:18-19). The last few verses of Revelation 7 provide a beautiful picture of what this will mean in eternity.

For the Lamb who stands in front of the throne will
be their Shepherd. He will lead them to the springs
of life-giving water. And God will wipe away all
their tears (Revelation 7:17).

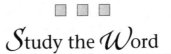

$\mathcal{S}$tudy the $\mathcal{W}$ord

1. Think back to the twentieth century (you remember
   the twentieth century, don't you?). Give at least one
   example of an event that was unleashed by each of
   the four horsemen.

   • *The first horseman*

   • *The second horseman*

   • *The third horseman*

   • *The fourth horseman*

Do you think the twenty-first century is going to be better or worse? Why?

2. Do you agree with the statement that the four horsemen represent God's mercy? Why or why not?

3. What does being martyred "for the word of God" and for being "faithful in their witness" mean (Revelation 6:9)?

Can you think of a modern-day martyr who fits that description?

4. Which view of the Great Tribulation do you most agree with? Give a scriptural reason for your answer.

5. Throughout the history of the church, martyrdom has been considered a privilege and suffering for Jesus an honor (see Acts 5:41). Do you think Christians in the Western world will ever have to deal with suffering and martyrdom? Why or why not?

6. Explain what asking God to remove you from the horrors of the Tribulation means.

    How do you prepare for difficult times?

7. Read Revelation 7:14-17. How does knowing that God is going to provide for our every need in heaven give you confidence when you face challenges now?

Chapter 8

The end draws near, my soul,
the end draws near;
Yet you do not care or make ready.
The time grows short, rise up;
the Judge is at the door.
The days of our life pass swiftly,
as a dream, as a flower.
Why do we trouble ourselves
over what is all in vain?

—Andrew of Crete

Revelation 7 was an interlude between Revelation 6, which described the breaking of the first six seals, and Revelation 8, which deals with the breaking of the seventh seal. The seventh seal is very significant because beneath this seal are the seven trumpet judgments.

This signals the beginning of new, more intense judgments by God against sin. In the next four chapters of Revelation, we're going to see the devastation heralded by the seven trumpets. We're also going to see the mercy and patience of God on full display.

The Seven Trumpets

Revelation 8–11

*R*evelation 8 begins with the Lamb breaking open the seventh seal, causing first silence and then thunder and lightning and a terrible earthquake. The seven angels with the seven trumpets are about to blow "their mighty blasts." Beginning in chapter 8, John sees a vision of supernatural plagues that are parallel to the plagues on Egypt. Only these plagues are worldwide and much more destructive than the plagues God sent against Pharaoh. The events set into motion by the seven trumpets clearly belong to God's final judgment of sin.

The First Four Trumpets (Revelation 8:6-13)

The first four trumpet judgments will bring the devastation of the world of nature as a warning for people to repent of their sins. God is going to actively and severely punish a world that has willfully opposed Him. By the time the first four trumpets have sounded, one-third of the earth will be destroyed:

- *The first trumpet*—One-third of the earth will burn.

- *The second trumpet*—One-third of the sea will turn to blood, effectively destroying one-third of everything in and on the sea.

- *The third trumpet*—One-third of the earth's fresh water will become bitter and undrinkable.

- *The fourth trumpet*—One-third of the light that shines on the earth—the sun, the moon, and the stars—will be extinguished. Eight hours of darkness will be added to each day.

Can you imagine the panic that will set in among the nations when these natural disasters occur? The Bible doesn't say exactly how all of this will be accomplished, but we have some clues. For example, after the second trumpet, "a great mountain of fire was thrown into the sea." Could this be a falling meteor or asteroid hitting the earth? Many scientists are concerned that this could happen to our planet.

God Is Being Patient

You would think that everyone who doesn't believe in Jesus Christ would turn to Him after these trumpet judgments. But just like Pharaoh refused to repent in the days of the Exodus when the ten plagues devastated Egypt, so the people on earth will defiantly turn their backs on God even in the face of severe judgment. Throughout human history God has done everything He can to encourage repentance. The Bible says that God is being patient for our sake. "He does not want anyone to perish, so he is giving more time for everyone to repent" (2 Peter 3:9). Yet someday God's patience will run out.

> *But the day of the Lord will come as unexpectedly as a thief. Then the heavens will pass away with a terrible noise, and everything in them will disappear in fire, and the earth and everything on it will be exposed to judgment* (2 Peter 3:10).

If you are a believer, thank God that you have repented. Then, pray for people you know who continue to refuse God. They still have time to repent, but someday that window of opportunity will close forever.

The Fifth Trumpet (Revelation 9:1-12)

As bad as the first four trumpets are, the fifth trumpet judgment is even worse. This trumpet will unleash demons from the Abyss who attack all the people who do not have "the seal of God on their foreheads." By contrast, all those who have the seal of God on their foreheads will be protected from these plagues, which will feature demonic locusts who sting but do not kill their victims. These monsters will be led by *Apollyon,* a powerful locust demon whose name means *destroyer.*

What Is the Abyss?

The Abyss, also known as the Bottomless Pit, is the dwelling place of the demonic forces. We know it's full of fire and smoke because that's what comes out when the angel opens it. The Abyss is also the eternal destination of those who have opposed God.

The Sixth Trumpet (Revelation 9:13-21)

Now things really get ugly. Woe to anyone alive at this time. The sixth trumpet will announce an army of 200 million mounted troops who will kill one-third of the world's population. Walvoord believes this will be a human army. Alan Johnson and others interpret this to mean 200 million demons. That doesn't mean that humans won't be involved in this horror of horrors, but the description of this unusually cruel and effective army is more consistent with the nature of demons. God's purpose in this is to help people "turn from their evil deeds." But still they will continue to "worship demons and idols," and they will refuse to repent.

More than half of the earth's population will be gone by the end of the sixth trumpet judgment. One-fourth will have died from the effects of the first four trumpet judgments, and one-third of those who remain will be killed from the sixth trumpet judgment. That means only 50 percent of the earth's population will be left before the beginning of the seventh trumpet judgment and the judgments of the seven bowls, which start in Revelation 15 (we'll cover this in chapter 10).

The Angel and the Small Scroll (Revelation 10)

The seventh trumpet judgment comes in Revelation 11:15. This trumpet triggers the seven bowls, which are described in Revelation 15. But before he gets to that, John sees another angel coming down from heaven holding a small scroll (Revelation 10). This scroll probably represents the revelations John is receiving. The angel asks John to eat the scroll, and at first it tastes like honey to him. This reminds us of David, who wrote: "How sweet are your words to my taste; they are sweeter than honey" (Psalm 119:103). Then, when John swallows the scroll, it makes his stomach sour.

Sweet and Sour

The Word of God should be sweet to us as we read it and meditate on it. But the Bible also contains information about the future of the human race that should turn our stomach because of the judgment to come. God wants us to have a heart for the lost. Just as Jesus grieved when His people rejected Him (Matthew 23:37-39), our hearts should break for those who have rejected Christ.

The Two Witnesses (Revelation 11)

Revelation 11:1-14 presents a section of prophecy that many scholars consider the most difficult in the entire book (and that's saying a lot). In this passage John refers to

- the temple, altar, and worshipers

- the holy city

- the two witnesses

- a period of 42 months, or 1260 days

Scholars have presented two main interpretations for these symbols. The one we prefer is that "the temple" refers to the Christian church and all believers. Peter refers to believers as a spiritual temple (1 Peter 2:5). The image of John measuring "the temple of God and the altar" and counting "the number of worshipers" seems to mean that God will protect and preserve His people. John is told that he should not measure the "outer courtyard," which will be trampled by the nations for 42 months. This could refer to the time during the Great Tribulation when the Antichrist will occupy Jerusalem, God's Holy City. Or it could refer to the community of believers, and the "trampling" could symbolize persecution.

The time period of "42 months" occurs only twice in Revelation—here in 11:2 and in 13:5, where it refers to the authority given to the beast for a period of 42 months. The time period of 1260 days is the same as 42 months (42 months x 30 days = 1260 days = 3½ years). The two witnesses (sometimes called the two prophets) are interpreted in many ways. The two main views are...

- They are two historical figures, such as Moses and Elijah, raised to life to prophesy to the Jews.

- They represent the witnessing church.

Whoever they are, the two witnesses seem to be literal people who will prophesy for 1260 days. God will protect them during this time, and their main purpose will be to call people to turn to God (that's always been the primary function of a prophet). At the end of the 1260 days, the witnesses will be killed by the beast coming out of the Abyss. The bodies of the witnesses will be left in the main street of Jerusalem for the world to stare at in celebration. For 3½ days the Antichrist and his followers will appear to have silenced the witnesses, but God will make their celebration brief. The two witnesses will be resurrected into heaven, striking terror into the hearts of God's enemies. At this point a terrible earthquake will come and destroy 7000 people.

The survivors of the earthquake will glorify God. This is consistent with what Paul wrote in Philippians 2:10: "At the name of Jesus every knee will bow, in heaven and on earth and under the earth." When Jesus finally triumphs over sin and evil and raises His people from the earth to be with Him in heaven forever, everyone—including unbelievers and demons—will be forced to bow to Him.

Study the Word

1. Immediately after the Lamb breaks the seventh seal, heaven is silent for half an hour. Evidently the only sounds are the prayers of God's people (Revelation 8:3). What is the value of silence in your relationship with God? See Psalm 46:10 and Isaiah 30:15.

2. The first four trumpets unleash worldwide disasters that impact nature in horribly destructive ways. Compare these "natural" end-time disasters with the natural disasters we see in our world today.

Do you think God causes the disasters we experience now, or do you think He permits these things to happen as nature takes its course? See Romans 8:21-22.

What about the future natural disasters? Will they be consequences of natural events, or will God cause them? Explain your answer.

3. The supernatural plagues described in Revelation 8–11 parallel the plagues of Egypt (see Exodus 7–11). What comfort can we take from the way the plagues of Egypt affected God's people?

4. If God uses judgment to encourage repentance, what has God done in your life to encourage you to repent?

5. The Bible says that God is holding off His final judgment so that more people have time to repent. Knowing this, should your witnessing tactics change? How?

6. The demons unleashed by the fifth and sixth trumpets exist today. Why don't we see this kind of demonic activity in the world right now?

What is the danger of dwelling too much on demons today?

What is the danger of dwelling too little on demons?

7. Has the Word of God ever turned your stomach? Why or why not?

Chapter 9

The Lord's body became a bait for death,
so that the dragon, hoping to swallow
him up, would be forced to disgorge with
him everyone else he had swallowed.

—*Cyril of Jerusalem*

At the end of Revelation 11, the seventh angel blows his trumpet, ushering in the seven bowl judgments. But before describing the final outpouring of God's wrath in Revelation 15 and 16, John witnesses an incredible drama of the ages, which he calls "an event of great significance." He is about to witness the great cosmic conflict between God and Satan—between good and evil. And we'll get to see this drama as it is played out before John's eyes in a Technicolor, multidimensional story.

John sees the root of all evil, sin, and suffering on the earth, and he comes to understand why the final battle between God and Satan at the end of the age must take place. God has hit the pause button in Revelation so John can witness the big picture. This is the greatest drama ever told, and we have a front-row seat in God's celestial cineplex.

An Epic Drama
for the Ages

Revelation 12–14

*T*he plot of this grand cosmic drama was well known in the ancient world. In fact, some elements of this plot are common to great stories to this day: An evil usurper who knows he is doomed plots to kill the yet-unborn prince who is destined to rule the kingdom. The prince's mother gives birth, and just as the usurper is about to seize his intended victim, the prince is snatched away and hidden in the desert until he is old enough to kill the usurper and claim his rightful kingdom. John tells the story with three main characters.

The Main Characters (Revelation 12:1-6)

The Woman

Some have thought the woman John sees represents Mary, but this powerful being is much more than a woman. She represents the nation of Israel, who gives birth to the Messiah (Isaiah 9:6-7; Micah 5:2). The Old Testament prophets pictured Israel as the wife of God (Isaiah 54:5-6; Jeremiah 3:6-8; Ezekiel 16:32; Hosea 2:16). The 12 stars on the woman's head represent the 12 tribes of Israel. Later in the story, the woman will symbolize all believers.

The birth of Jesus takes on new meaning in the context of this epic drama between God and Satan. We can celebrate the familiar story by singing carols and exchanging gifts, but we need to recognize that the birth of the Messiah is much bigger than a story we think about once a year. When Jesus was born, the entire universe was shaken to its core. We know the multitudes of angels rejoiced, but we also must be aware that Satan put his dark army on notice, for the one who will eventually crush them had come to earth.

The Dragon

The dragon is Satan (as we will see in 12:9), a fierce and marauding foe who is the enemy of the woman and her unborn child. His power is so great that his sweeping tail drags down one-third of the stars. The dragon is ready to devour the child the moment He is born because Satan has known all along that the coming Messiah will eventually crush him (God revealed this in Genesis 3:15 right after the human race fell into sin through Satan's temptation).

Satan pursued Jesus throughout His earthly ministry, attempting to kill Him at least three times: once shortly after Jesus was born, when King Herod ordered the slaughtering of every baby boy under the age of two (Matthew 2:16-18); once during his temptation of Jesus when he tried to convince Jesus to jump off the highest point of the Temple in Jerusalem (Matthew 4:5); and once when Jesus was crucified (Matthew 27:50). As we will see in Revelation 16, Satan will try once again to kill Jesus as he mobilizes the demonic forces of evil and the armies of the earth against the conquering King in the greatest battle in history.

The Child

This is Jesus the Messiah, who was born to the nation of Israel to rule the kingdom but had to be whisked away to the wilderness before Herod could kill Him. Some interpreters see this as symbolic. The wilderness represents a place of spiritual refuge and growth. Throughout Scripture the wilderness is a place where God's people go for reflection, renewal, and safety. It's where God speaks to His own. Moses spent 40 years in the wilderness. John the Baptist lived in the wilderness before beginning his public ministry to Israel (Luke 1:80). And Jesus was tempted by Satan in the wilderness (Matthew 4:1).

The War in Heaven (Revelation 12:7-17)

This section expands on the drama and explains how Satan was thrown out of heaven. The cosmic struggle that Michael and his angels fight against Satan and his angels is very real (Ephesians 6:12). This epic battle of biblical proportions took place in eternity past, but it hasn't stopped Satan from fighting God, His Son, and His people.

Your Battle Is Christ's Battle

The battle between God and Satan is also the battle between Jesus and Satan for two reasons: 1) God and Jesus are one, and 2) Jesus, the Savior of the world, came to conquer sin, Satan, and death. When you receive Jesus as your Savior and Lord, you become one of God's eternal children. But you also become an enemy of Satan, who is Christ's enemy. You are literally on the front lines of the spiritual battle between good and evil. Not to worry. Even though you may have difficult days, the victory is secure because of Christ's love for you (Romans 8:38-39).

Satan popped up in the Garden of Eden disguised as a snake and tempted God's created beings, causing them to rebel. God cursed Satan by telling him that an offspring of the woman would crush his head (Genesis 3:15). When that offspring—Jesus the Messiah—came to live on the earth as a man, Satan tried to kill Him, but death could not hold Him in the grave. Jesus conquered sin and death, and once again Satan was defeated.

Satan knows he is doomed to a third and final defeat, but he hasn't given up. A voice shouting across heaven recaps the story:

> *It has happened at last—the salvation and power and kingdom of our God, and the authority of his Christ! For the Accuser has been thrown down to earth—the one who accused our brothers and sisters before our God day and night. And they have*

> *defeated him because of the blood of the Lamb and because of their testimony. And they were not afraid to die. Rejoice, O heavens! And you who live in the heavens, rejoice! But terror will come on the earth and the sea. For the Devil has come down to you in great anger, and he knows that he has little time* (Revelation 12:10-11).

Even though Satan knows he is doomed to defeat, he continues to fight God and God's people. Why? Because he wants to take as many people with him as possible.

Our friend Jon Courson says Satan is like the guy standing on the edge of a swimming pool. A bunch of people decide to gang up on the guy and push him in, and there's no question that he is going in the pool. But as he goes in, he grabs and claws and takes as many people with him as he possibly can. This is what Satan is doing. He knows he's going down, but while he can still fight, he is taking as many people with him as he can.

The Two Beasts (Revelation 13)

A big part of Satan's final attempt to defeat God, the Prince, and God's people is described in Revelation 13. Here the two great beasts are revealed:

The Beast from the Sea (Revelation 13:1-10)

This is the Antichrist, who gets his power directly from Satan. Easley calls the Antichrist "an evil parody of the Christ of God." The goal of Satan and the Antichrist is to persuade people to worship them rather than God. Paul describes this dangerous fraud this way:

> *This evil man will come to do the work of Satan with counterfeit power and signs and miracles. He*

will use every kind of wicked deception to fool
those who are on their way to destruction because
they refuse to believe the truth that would save
them (2 Thessalonians 2:9-10).

The Beast from the Earth (Revelation 13:11-18)

Satan also empowers the beast known as the "false prophet" to be the Antichrist's sidekick. Through demonic miracles, the false prophet will create an entire religion devoted to worshiping the Antichrist. The false prophet will administer the "mark of the beast," which is some form of identification placed on the forehead or right hand by which the people display their allegiance to the Antichrist. Without this identification, no one can buy or sell in the world's economy.

The Lamb and the 144,000 (Revelation 14:1-5)

Revelation 13 shows the horror unleashed by Satan and his evil cohorts, the Antichrist, and the false prophet. It's a bleak picture. Revelation 14 reveals the eternal future for those who have been sealed by God. In contrast to the unbelievers who received the mark of the beast, this group of 144,000—representing the complete number of all who believe in Christ—have the mark of God on their foreheads (7:4). They are characterized as...

- spiritually undefiled

- pure as virgins

- following the Lamb wherever He goes

- purchased from among the people on the earth as a special offering to God

- blameless and without falsehood

*W*hat's the *S*ignificance of 666?

Through the ages people have tried to figure out the identity of the Antichrist based on the number 666, the mark of the beast. About all we know about the number is that it represents imperfection, as compared to the perfect number, 777.

One More Chance (Revelation 14:6-13)

Even at this late stage when the final judgment is about to begin, God offers a chance for people to turn to Him. He does the same now, and He will do the same at the midnight hour. Anyone can repent—that is, until the time God begins to judge the world for the final time.

The Great Harvest (Revelation 14:14-20)

The famous first verse of the "Battle Hymn of the Republic" goes like this:

> Mine eyes have seen the glory of the coming of the Lord;
>
> He is trampling out the vintage where the grapes of wrath are stored;
>
> He hath loosed the fateful lightning of His terrible swift sword;
>
> His truth is marching on.

Julia Ward Howe, the composer of that stirring song, took her imagery of the grapes of wrath from this section in Revelation. This is God's final judgment of sin. All people will be harvested with God's mighty sickle. God's people will be taken to heaven, and God's enemies will be sent to eternal punishment.

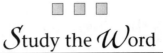

$\mathcal{S}$tudy the $\mathcal{W}$ord

1. Can you think of another story in modern times that parallels the great drama told in Revelation 12? Why might God's cosmic story resemble so many other stories?

2. Why is a story such a powerful way to tell the truth about something? Who is the greatest storyteller you know? What is the greatest storybook?

3. Was Satan responsible for killing Jesus in the crucifixion? If not, who killed Jesus?

What would have happened if Jesus had not died? See Romans 5:6-11.

4. Have you ever had a wilderness experience? What happened?

5. What defense do we have against Satan, our great Accuser? List at least three things we can do to defend ourselves against Satan and his demonic forces. Use Scripture to support your answers.

6. Why will people be so attracted to the Antichrist if he's such an evil person? See Daniel 8:23-25.

7. Read Revelation 14:6-7. In what ways is this message relevant to us today?

8. Compare the harvest described in Revelation 14:15-16 with the harvest described in 14:17-20. What do these two harvests represent?

Chapter 10

Great and marvelous are your actions,
Lord God Almighty.
Just and true are your ways,
O King of the nations.
Who will not fear, O Lord,
and glorify your name?
For you alone are holy.
All nations will come and
worship before you,
for your righteous deeds have
been revealed.

—*Revelation 15:3-4*

Is your mind reeling with all of the images, symbols, and events of Revelation? Just think of what John experienced. The whirlwind of visions must have shocked his senses and stirred his heart as he witnessed the awesome plan and power of God unfolding step-by-step.

Before we dive into the next chapter, let's review where we've been. We're still in the second vision that began in Revelation 4:1. Everything since then has focused on Jesus, who is the theme of Revelation, and the events leading up to His Second Coming. Thanks to God's revelation and John's detailed descriptions, we've seen...

- glimpses of heaven's throne room and the worship of the Lamb

- the opening of the seven seals

- the seven trumpet judgments and the beginning of the Great Tribulation

- an epic drama that tells us why these things are happening

Now we're going to see the beginning of the end as the final phase of God's judgment unfolds through the seven bowls. Hang on. Things are about to heat up in a big way.

The Seven Bowls and the Fall of Babylon

Revelation 15–18

*A*s if the last "event of great significance"—the epic drama of Revelation 12—wasn't dramatic enough, John witnesses another "significant event" beginning in Revelation 15. On a crystal sea mixed with fire, John sees "all the people who had been victorious over the beast." They are holding harps given to them by God and are singing the song of Moses and the song of the Lamb.

The song of Moses (Exodus 15) was originally sung after God delivered His people from Pharaoh and his army. Moses led the people in a song of praise to the God who saved them. Now, at the end of the age, God's people are once again singing a praise song to God, who delivered them from the beast and his army. Following this remarkable sight, John witnesses the final judgments of God, the seven bowls.

The seven bowls, which are unleashed by the seventh trumpet, are the last plagues to come to planet earth. These bowl judgments will bring about the complete destruction of evil and will end the wicked reign of the Antichrist. Revelation 15, which picks up where Revelation 11 left off, connects to Revelation 16, where the pouring of the bowls begins.

The Seven Bowls (Revelation 15–16)

After witnessing the heavenly praise service in 15:1-4, John peers into the Tabernacle of God and sees seven angels. One of the "four living beings" then hands each one of the angels "a gold bowl filled with the terrible wrath of God." About this section, John Walvoord writes:

> Taken as a whole, Revelation 15:5-8 presents a fearful picture of impending divine judgment on a wicked world. The judgments which are poured out in Revelation 16 fully justify this ominous introduction.

If you're keeping track of these events chronologically, the seven bowls of God's wrath described in Revelation 16 occur at the end of the Great Tribulation and close to the time of the Second Coming. Because the destruction of these judgments is so severe, the bowls are likely to be poured out quickly. Yet the effects of each bowl do not end quickly. Truly this will be a terrible time to be on planet earth. Here's a summary of the seven bowls:

Bowl 1—*Malignant sores break out on everyone who has the mark of the beast.*

Notice that God's wrath comes only to unbelievers, those who have the mark of the beast (13:16) and worship his statue (13:14-15). According to the pretribulational and midtribulational viewpoints, no believers will be on the earth at this time. The posttribulational theory teaches that believers are still present during these awful judgments, but they will be protected by the seal of Christ (7:3) and Christ's personal guarantee (3:10).

Bowl 2—*The sea turns to blood and everything in it dies.*

During the second trumpet judgment, one-third of the sea became blood. Now the entire sea becomes "like the blood of a corpse," killing everything in it. Clearly God's patience and mercy have run out. The opportunity for second chances is gone.

Bowl 3—*All the fresh water turns to blood.*

Now all the fresh water burns to blood. All the water on planet earth is completely contaminated. Next to breathable air, the most basic need for human survival is drinkable water, and now that is gone.

Bowl 4—*The sun burns people, yet they curse God.*

The fourth trumpet blocked the sun, moon, and stars for 8 hours a day. The fourth bowl has the opposite effect and creates a blast of heat from the sun. Once again, if believers are on the earth at this time, they will be protected (7:14-16), but the unbelievers will be scorched. Still, they will refuse to repent because their hearts are completely turned away from God.

*I*s *T*his *O*verkill?

At this point you may be thinking that God is going just a bit overboard (even though you really know He could never do anything improper or unjust). Is killing humanity in this way really necessary? Why not just get it over quickly rather than torturing people in such a manner? Don't feel bad about having such questions. At the same time, don't look too far for an answer. In Revelation 16:5-6 the angel with authority over all water makes a bold and affirming declaration: "You are just in sending this judgment, O Holy One, who is and who always was. For your holy people and your prophets have been killed, and their blood was poured out on the earth. So you have given their murderers blood to drink. It is their just reward." God is the ultimate Judge in a universe that He created, and He has every right to deliver justice in any manner He chooses.

Bowl 5—Darkness covers the entire earth, yet the people refuse to repent.

This isn't like the partial darkness that comes from the fifth trumpet; this is complete darkness, just like the plague of darkness that gripped Egypt (Exodus 10:23). Anyone alive at this time is suffering from malignant sores and severe burns, yet there is none who repent. The total depravity of the human race is on full display.

Bowl 6—The Euphrates River dries up, allowing the armies of the East to march to the west for the battle of Armageddon.

This is the first mention in Revelation of Armageddon, the last great battle of Satan's forces and the armies of the earth against God. The natural boundary of the Euphrates River is now gone, allowing the armies from the East, together with the rulers of the world, to march into battle. Ironically, these armies will be enticed to their final judgment and destruction by Satan, the beast, and the false prophet.

---

*A*rmageddon: the *R*eal *D*oomsday

The final event of the Tribulation will be the battle of Armageddon. Before John wrote about it in Revelation, this battle was predicted by the prophets Daniel, Joel, and Zechariah. Armageddon is going to be a battle unlike anything the world has ever known. Military powers from the four corners of the globe will converge on a large plain in northern Israel to battle for world domination. Because the land of Palestine and the capital city of Jerusalem will become the center of world power by the end of the Tribulation, we should not be surprised that the final battle of the ages will occur here. As we will see in Revelation 19:11-21, the battle will be won by Jesus Christ, who will come as a rider on a white horse.

Bowl 7—The great cities of the world are destroyed.

As soon as this last bowl is poured out, God shouts from heaven, "It is finished!" The greatest earthquake in history then rocks the world. Indeed, history is finished. The end of the world has come. God's wrath has been completely poured out.

The Great Prostitute and the Fall of Babylon (Revelation 17–18)

The great prostitute has been interpreted to mean the Roman Empire, and this was undoubtedly what the first-century Christians thought. However, from our perspective, the prostitute represents any system or civilization that opposes God. At the end of the Tribulation, the Antichrist (fully empowered by Satan) will have succeeded in uniting the entire world against God. His charisma and power will convince many people to join him. The "ten horns and ten kings" (17:12) represent nations yet to come. This could be a literal number, or it may represent the totality with which the Antichrist will persuade the nations of the earth to oppose God. The only purpose of this anti-alliance will be to wage war against the Lamb.

The first-century Christians were correct in identifying Rome as the woman John saw in his vision (17:18). Rome was known for its idolatry and persecution of Christians. But Rome isn't the only empire that shook its fist at God. Throughout history, many nations and kingdoms have openly defied and opposed God. Ancient Rome was no different from Egypt and Babylon in this regard. And in the past century we witnessed the rise and fall of the Soviet Union, which President Ronald Reagan called the "evil empire." He was completely correct in his assessment, for nations such as these are moved and motivated by Satan to resist and oppose God. And yet even ancient Rome and atheistic states like it are merely a foretaste of the alliance of nations that will form against God and His people at the end of the Great Tribulation.

Revelation 18 describes the total destruction of all those people, nations, and civilizations that oppose God. God will do this by destroying the commerce, religion, and culture of every wicked and rebellious system on the planet. The past great civilizations of Babylon and Rome and the future civilizations of the Antichrist will disappear like a boulder thrown into the ocean.

Study the Word

1. Read the song of the Lamb (Revelation 15:3-4). Why can't we sing this now?

   Will we ever be able to sing it before Christ comes again?

2. As human beings, we are tempted to think that God must operate by our standards of justice rather than His own. Write a paragraph explaining why God's methods of dealing with His creation and His created beings are consistent with His nature. See Job 38:1-4 and 40:6-9; Psalm 103:8-13; and Isaiah 55:6-9.

3. Revelation 16:9 includes an incredible description: "Everyone was burned by this blast of heat, and they cursed the name of God, who sent all of these plagues." Make an application to someone living today who believes they have been burned by God.

Have you ever felt burned by God? Did it make you angry? When is anger toward God a good thing?

When is anger toward God a very bad thing?

4. How can a person develop a "hard heart" toward God and not repent, no matter what happens? See Hebrews 6:4-6.

5. In Revelation 16:14 John writes about "that great judgment day of God Almighty," also known as "the day of the Lord." In what way are we living in the day of the Lord right now?

6. The references to *Armageddon* in literature and film are too numerous to count. Give one example and give two reasons why the allusion to the real Armageddon is valid.

7. Read Revelation 16:17 and compare the phrase, "It is finished" with the words of Jesus in John 19:30 and Matthew 27:50-53. Make a list of the similarities between the two events.

8. Are any governments, nations, or kingdoms in existence today openly opposed to God?

Chapter 11

The return of Christ is a *fundamental doctrine* of the Christian faith. It is embodied in hymns of hope; it forms the climax of the creeds; it is the sublime motive for evangelistic and missionary activity and daily it is voiced in the inspired prayer: "Even so, come, Lord Jesus."

—Charles R. Erdman

Beginning with Revelation 19, the tone and the content of John's visions shift dramatically. If Revelation were a classic three-act play, we would be done with the crisis phase of Act II, and the curtain would now be going up on Act III. This is the climax of the story—God's story—and it couldn't be more glorious.

As our study races through these final four chapters of Revelation, here's what we're going to see:

- Heaven's Victory Song (Revelation 19)

- God's Kingdom on Earth (Revelation 20)

- Heaven: Our Final Home (Revelation 21)

- Jesus Is Coming Soon! (Revelation 22)

So set your imagination on "stunned." The things you're going to study now are out of this world.

The King Is Coming

Revelation 19

*J*esus Christ is the central point of human history, and the Second Coming of Christ is the climactic event. When Jesus comes to earth again, all sin and evil will be defeated forever. The first time Jesus came to earth, He was the suffering servant. When He comes again, He will be...

- the Bridegroom dressed for the world's greatest wedding feast

- the Mighty Warrior ready to do battle against those who oppose Him

- the Reigning King who will rule the earth for a thousand years

- the Supreme Judge who will reward the faithful and sentence His enemies

- the Host of Heaven, where all believers will live forever

Heaven's Victory Song (Revelation 19:1-5)

Revelation 19 opens with John witnessing a vast crowd singing:

> *Hallelujah! Salvation is from our God. Glory and power belong to him alone. His judgments are just and true. He has punished the great prostitute who corrupted the earth with her immorality, and he has avenged the murder of his servants* (19:1-2).

This is the biblical version of the "Hallelujah Chorus." Since we tend to hear Handel's great oratorio at Christmastime, people assume that the great composer had that in mind when he wrote it in 1741. Actually, Handel meant for the *Messiah* to be performed at Easter time, and the famous "Hallelujah Chorus" (the one where people stand the moment the first notes are played) is all about Christ's final victory over sin and death. This famous line from the "Hallelujah Chorus" is taken directly from the King James Version of Revelation 19:6:

> *For the Lord God omnipotent reigneth.*

The word *Hallelujah,* which means "Praise God," occurs only four times in the New Testament, and they are all in Revelation 19. So the next time you hear the "Hallelujah Chorus" from Handel's *Messiah,* think of the thunderous praise and worship meeting in heaven announcing the coming King of kings and Lord of lords.

The Wedding Feast (19:6-10)

The 24 elders and the 4 living beings are back doing what they do best—worshiping God. In addition, all of heaven is preparing "the wedding feast of the Lamb." The table in heaven is being set for the bride of Christ. Soon the church—the family of God—will join the Bridegroom in a grand and glorious wedding.

The Bible uses the metaphor of a bridegroom and a bride to illustrate the love Jesus has for the church. Paul wrote to the Corinthians: "I am jealous for you with the jealousy of God himself. For I promised you as a pure bride to one husband, Christ" (2 Corinthians 11:2). As a believer, you are the bride of Christ, who is coming back for you. Right now the church and Christ are engaged, and the Holy Spirit is like the engagement ring guaranteeing that the bridegroom will return (2 Corinthians 1:21-22). That's why this image in Revelation of a wedding feast being prepared is so appropriate.

Do You Have Your Invitation?

You don't just "crash" a wedding dinner. You have to be invited. The Bible clearly says that only those "who are invited to the wedding feast of the Lamb" (19:9) will be able to go. These are all believers throughout the ages and from every nation who have trusted Jesus Christ for their salvation. The angel calls them "blessed." Each time this "beatitude" is used (there are seven beatitudes or "blesseds" in Revelation—1:3; 14:13; 16:15; 19:9; 20:6; 22:7; 22:14), it describes the "blessedness" of those who are faithful to Christ.

The Second Coming (Revelation 19:11-21)

No doubt you've been to lots of weddings. You've seen how the bridegroom walks out to the stage from a door on the side, often with his best man and the pastor behind him. The groom is usually grinning as he anticipates his bride, who will soon be walking down the aisle. It's cute, charming, and tender, but not very dramatic. And it bears no resemblance to the entrance Jesus will make when He comes as the Bridegroom for His bride, the church. Here's what it will be like:

> Then I saw heaven opened, and a white horse was standing there. And the one sitting on the horse was named Faithful and True. For he judges fairly and then goes to war. His eyes were bright like flames of fire, and on his head were many crowns. A name was written on him, and only he knew what it meant. He was clothed with a robe dipped in blood, and his title was the Word of God (Revelation 19:11-13).

That's it, folks. This is the Second Coming, and if you are a believer, you will be among "the armies of heaven, dressed in pure white linen" following Him on white horses. But you won't need to fight. Jesus Christ will defeat the armies of Satan single-handedly with the sharp sword that comes from His mouth. Both the Antichrist and the false prophet will be "thrown alive into the lake of fire that burns with sulfur." That will be an awesome sight.

The Moment We've Been Waiting For

When describing the Second Coming to His disciples, Jesus explained, "No one knows the day or the hour when these things will happen" (Matthew 24:36). Unbelievers will be taken completely off guard, but as believers we should be expecting the return of Christ to earth. Jesus told His disciples exactly what's going to happen:

You will see me, the Son of Man, sitting at God's right hand in the place of power and coming back on the clouds of heaven (Mark 14:62).

Shortly after Jesus ascended into heaven after His crucifixion and resurrection, an angel also told the disciples:

Jesus has been taken away from you into heaven. And someday, just as you saw him go, he will return! (Acts 1:11).

And just so there wouldn't be any doubt as to what was going to happen, the apostle Paul wrote this about the Second Coming of Jesus:

And God will provide rest for you who are being persecuted and also for us when the Lord Jesus appears from heaven. He will come with his mighty angels, in flaming fire, bringing judgment on those who don't know God and on those who refuse to obey the Good News of our Lord Jesus (2 Thessalonians 1:7-8).

The Nature of the Second Coming

Besides being glorious for believers and horrible for unbelievers, what will the Second Coming be like? Theologians list five characteristics:

1. The Second Coming will be personal.

Just as Jesus left the earth in person, He will return in His resurrected, recognizable body (Acts 1:11).

2. *The Second Coming will be* physical.

Because Jesus will come to earth in His body, everyone will see Him (Revelation 1:7).

3. *The Second Coming will be* visible.

The whole world will see His coming whether they want to or not (Colossians 3:4).

4. *The Second Coming will be* sudden.

You would think that after the events of the Tribulation and Armageddon, people would be counting the days for the return of Christ. But the Bible tells us that people will be deluded by the Antichrist and will be caught by surprise at the sudden return of Christ (1 Thessalonians 5:1-2).

5. *The Second Coming will be* glorious and triumphant.

Jesus came to earth the first time in obscurity (Isaiah 53:2-3). His next coming will be magnificent (Matthew 24:30).

A Place Called Hell

In Revelation 19:20 we read that both the beast and the false prophet are thrown into "the lake of fire that burns with sulfur." This is the same "hell" that Jesus talked about in Matthew 18:9 and Mark 9:43. Some interpreters see the image of a "lake of fire" as a metaphor for eternal separation from God (2 Thessalonians 1:9), while others view the flames and the sulfur as literal. However hell turns out to be, it will be a horrible place of eternal torment and agony that is reserved for the beast and the false prophet (Revelation 19:20), Satan (20:10), death and the grave (20:14), and anyone whose name is not found recorded in the Book of Life (20:15).

■ ■ ■

*S*tudy the *W*ord

1. Make a list of five characteristics of the first coming of Jesus Christ to earth. Do the same thing for the Second Coming of Christ. Why do you think Jesus will have come to earth in two such different ways?

2. What is the reason why the crowds and beings in heaven shout "Hallelujah!" in each of these four verses?

    •   19:1

    •   19:3

    •   19:4

    •   19:6

3. Have you already received and responded to your invitation to the wedding feast of the Lamb? Is the wedding feast guest list already full, or do others still have time to receive and respond to an invitation? What role should you play in this process?

4. Read the description of the Second Coming again in Revelation 19:11-16. Now read 1 Thessalonians 4:15-18, a passage of Scripture describing the Rapture. Discuss how the Rapture and the Second Coming could be two separate events or a single event.

5. Read Revelation 19:11-16. Write out the descriptions given of the returning Christ. If possible, find another verse of Scripture that parallels each of these descriptions (don't forget to look back at Revelation 1:12-16).

6. Read Matthew 24:37-39, where Jesus compares His Second Coming to the Flood in Noah's day. How will the Second Coming be like the Flood? How will it be different?

Why will unbelievers be so unprepared for the Second Coming?

How can believers be better prepared?

7. Is believing that hell is a place of fire and sulfur (as opposed to a place of eternal suffering but not a literal lake of fire) important?

Chapter 12

What a mighty thing it is to live for God's kingdom! Live for it; look for it—it is so powerful it will completely overwhelm you.

—*J. Heinrich Arnold*

Revelation 19 clearly teaches that Jesus will come in glory and power in order to reveal Himself and His own and to judge the beast, the false prophet, and their armies. In Revelation 20 we learn some additional reasons why Jesus is coming back a second time:

- to bind Satan

- to judge the nations

- to deliver and bless creation

- to set up His kingdom

All of these things found in Revelation 20 are pretty straightforward except for the kingdom. Ever since Revelation was written, people have debated the meaning of the "thousand years" described in this chapter. We're going to consider the meaning of this so-called Millennial Kingdom, along with the implications of Satan's final defeat and the Great White Throne judgment.

God's Kingdom on Earth

Revelation 20

*T*he next great event in the end-times countdown will be the Millennium, a thousand-year period of time when Christ will rule in a literal kingdom on earth. At least that's one view of the Millennium. Let's look at the three main interpretations:

Premillennialism

This literal view holds that Christ will return before (that's where the *pre* comes from) the Millennium. (Another way of looking at it is that the Millennium will immediately follow the Second Coming.) After defeating the armies of Satan, Jesus will rule from His throne in Jerusalem, and Satan will be bound in the bottomless pit for the entire time. The final judgment will come at the conclusion of the Millennium, followed by eternity.

---

*W*hat's a *M*illennium?

The word *Millennium* never appears in the Bible. It comes from the Latin words *mille,* meaning "thousand," and *annus,* meaning "year." The phrase "thousand years" is found six times in Revelation 20.

Amillennialism

This view teaches that there will be no future, literal 1000-year reign of Christ on earth (*a* means "no") squeezed in between Christ's return and the final judgment. In fact, we are currently living in a millennial state on earth in a spiritual kingdom—God's kingdom. This is what Jesus meant when He said, "Make the Kingdom of God your primary concern" (Matthew 6:33).

Postmillennialism

Those who hold this view believe the church is in the process of building the kingdom of God right now by being a positive influence (salt and light) in society. The term *postmillennialism* simply means that Christ will return *after* such a kingdom has been established. The primary part of this view is its belief in the final triumph of good over evil before Christ returns. When Jesus does return, this age will end and eternity will begin.

A Literal and a Spiritual Kingdom

Whatever your view on the Millennium, recognize that the kingdom of God is both a *literal* and a *spiritual* kingdom. Jesus will literally rule during the Millennium, and His rule will extend into eternity after that. But He has a spiritual kingdom as well. Alva J. McClain calls it the "inner and therefore unseen rule of God over the hearts of men who yield themselves to His will." Are you allowing Jesus to rule in your heart right now, just as He will someday rule the earth? Are you making the kingdom of God your primary concern?

Why Believe in a Literal Millennium?

We think there are three reasons for believing in a literal Millennium:

- A literal Millennium fulfills the *promises of God,* including His promise to Abraham that his descendents would be a great nation in a literal land (Genesis 15:18-21).

- A literal Millennium fulfills the *purpose of Christ* in coming back to earth to set up His literal kingdom (Matthew 25:31).

- A literal Millennium fulfills the *promise of Scripture* of a period during which peace and righteousness will reign upon the earth (Isaiah 2:4).

The Binding of Satan (Revelation 20:1-3)

One of the key aspects of Revelation 20 occurs in the first three verses. An angel comes down from heaven and puts a heavy chain on Satan—the dragon, "that old serpent, the

Devil"—and throws him into a bottomless pit for a thousand years. This coincides, of course, with the thousand-year reign of Christ.

Satan is not completely free in our present world (thanks to the restraining influence of the Holy Spirit), but he is very busy causing trouble for unbelievers and believers alike. Satan's relentless and destructive activities today include...

- binding the minds of those who don't believe (2 Corinthians 4:4)

- deceiving people by disguising himself as an angel of light (2 Corinthians 11:14)

- working in the hearts of those who refuse to obey God (Ephesians 2:2)

- hindering the work of missionaries (1 Thessalonians 2:18)

- harassing and attacking unsuspecting believers (1 Peter 5:8)

In the Millennium, Satan will be completely bound, perhaps to give the nations on earth a glimpse of what heaven will be like.

What Will the Millennium Be Like?
(Revelation 20:4-6)

Theologians offer several characteristics of the literal future Millennium:

1. Jesus will personally rule from the throne of David in Jerusalem. This fulfills God's promise to David that his kingdom would continue forever (2 Samuel 7:16).

2. *The church will reign with Christ.* As the bride of Christ (Revelation 21:9), the church—which is made up of all believers—will reign with Christ over the Gentile world (2 Timothy 2:12).

3. *Israel will be completely regathered and will recognize its King.* The people of Israel, God's chosen people, will be regathered and will become a great nation, just as God promised (Isaiah 11:10-13) and Jesus predicted (Matthew 24:30-31).

4. *The nations of the earth will populate the Millennium.* Jesus told His disciples of a time when He would judge the living nations on earth before the Millennium (these would be people who survive the Tribulation). He will separate the sheep from the goats (Matthew 25:31-46). The sheep will evidently be those who accepted Christ during the Tribulation, and the goats will be those who continued to reject Him. The sheep will be a part of the Millennial Kingdom.

5. *Satan will be out of the picture during the Millennium.* There's no debate here. Satan will be captured, bound, and thrown into the Abyss for a thousand years. We can only imagine how glorious this time will be with Jesus in charge and Satan in chains.

6. *Nature will be restored to near perfection.* The earth will be in pretty bad shape after the Tribulation and Armageddon. When Christ reigns on earth, nature will be restored and delivered from the curse of sin.

7. *Conditions will be heavenly.* The Millennium won't be heaven (that comes later), but it will be as close to heaven on earth as possible. For a beautiful description of what life will be like, read Isaiah 65:21-25.

Satan's Last Gasp (Revelation 20:7-10)

Satan must be a bigger fool than we give him credit for. The Bible says that at the conclusion of the Millennium, Satan will be let out of his prison. He will foolishly try to mount yet another rebellion against God and His people. This will literally be his last gasp. After his brief insurrection, Satan will be defeated, crushed, judged, and sentenced forever.

The Great White Throne (Revelation 20:11-15)

The Great White Throne judgment is for all people who have rejected God's plan of salvation. They are unquestionably guilty. God knows those who belong to Him because their names are written in the Book of Life. At this judgment, the Book of Life will be opened, and the names of the unbelievers will not be found inside. Jesus Himself will say: "I don't know you. Go away" (Luke 13:27). Following this, they will join the Antichrist, the false prophet, and Satan in the lake of fire, also known as hell.

Will Believers Be Judged?

Yes, but their judgment is not going to involve any penalties (Romans 8:1). The judgment of Christians is called the "judgment seat of Christ" (Romans 14:10 KJV). The Greek word for "judgment seat" is *bema,* which represented the judge's bench at the Olympic stadium in ancient Greece. When an athlete won the race, he stepped up onto the *bema* to receive an award. Similarly, Christians will have to give a "personal account" to the Lord (Romans 14:12), but not to review our sins. Rather, it will be an examination of the quality of our service to God. First Corinthians 3:10-15 clearly teaches that some of the things we do for Christ will have value, like jewels, while other things we do are nothing more than junk to God. Jewels will be rewarded at the judgment seat; junk will not.

$\mathcal{S}$tudy the $\mathcal{W}$ord

1. Do you think holding a particular view regarding the Millennium is important? Why or why not?

2. If you believe in a literal Millennium, what do you think are the main reasons why Jesus is going to set up His earthly kingdom before inviting all believers into His eternal heaven?

3. What are some ways that you can make the kingdom of God your top priority right now? What prevents you from doing these things?

4. We know that God is greater than Satan, and Revelation 20:1-3 shows us that God can bind Satan anytime He chooses. Why doesn't God bind Satan right now?

Why do you think God is waiting until the end of the Millennium to bind Satan for good?

5. What is your best defense against Satan right now? Use Scripture to support your answer.

6. What is the importance of believers improving the quality of their service to Christ?

What can you do now to increase your chances of having some jewels to present to Christ when you stand before Him in the *bema* seat?

7. Read Revelation 20:4. Will the martyrs receive a special reward from Christ? Do you think this could motivate some people to be willing to die for Christ?

Chapter 13

If heaven is not real, every honest person
will disbelieve in it simply for that reason,
however desirable it is, and if it is real,
every honest man, woman, child, scientist,
theologian, saint, and sinner will want to
believe in it simply because it is real,
not just because it is desirable.

—*C.S. Lewis*

Congratulations! You've worked your way through Revelation, and now you've come to the payoff. If you are like us, you probably feel as if you've been hacking your way through a jungle with your spiritual machete. We've tried to guide you as best we can, showing you the various points of interest and warning signs along the way. We hope you are wiser. We hope you have grown to have a greater appreciation and reverence for our sovereign God and His precious Son, Jesus Christ.

Now your journey is almost complete, and the best part is right ahead of you. In this final chapter you're going to burst from the jungle and see an almost unimaginable sight: a new heaven, a new earth, and the New Jerusalem. This is heaven, your final home, and it's not far off because Jesus is coming soon!

Heaven: Our Final Home

Revelation 21–22

Some of the sweetest and most reassuring words Jesus ever spoke while He was on earth were recorded by John in his Gospel:

Don't be troubled. You trust God, now trust in me. There are many rooms in my Father's home, and I am going to prepare a place for you. If this were not so, I would tell you plainly. When everything is

> *ready, I will come and get you, so that you will always be with me where I am* (John 14:1-3).

Isn't that incredible? Jesus is preparing a place in heaven for all those who have trusted in Him. Revelation 21 describes just a portion of what heaven will be like, and even these 27 verses only scratch the surface. Yet they tell us a lot about this glorious place waiting for all believers through the ages. We would encourage you to sit down right now in a quiet place and read Revelation 21. Let the images fill your mind and your heart. Reflect on the beauty and grandeur of heaven, and then realize that you are only capturing a fraction of what Jesus has prepared for you. As C.S. Lewis writes:

> Your place in heaven will seem to be made for you and you alone, because you were made for it.

The last time humankind lived in a perfect environment and in perfect harmony with God was in the Garden of Eden. Since then we've lived in an environment that is less than perfect (and sometimes downright hostile), and we've been enemies of God. Our only hope has been that the person and work of Jesus Christ will give us salvation. But what a hope that is for us, because through Christ and Christ alone, we have the hope of spending eternity in heaven, where we will live in a perfect place and in a perfect relationship with our Creator. Is that possible? Is that a dream, or is heaven for real?

Heaven Is for Real

Some people prefer to think of heaven as a state of mind. Don't fall into this trap. Heaven is a real place that will exist forever. Gary Habermas writes that "the life of heaven is eternal life." And it isn't merely a continuation of our life now. There will be "no more death or sorrow or crying or pain. For the old world and its evils are gone forever" (Revelation 21:4).

Heaven won't be a boring place where you pluck a harp while sitting on a fluffy cloud. In heaven, true believers will see Jesus face-to-face and be able to interact with Him (1 John 3:2). We will serve God (Revelation 5:10) and give praise to Jesus, the Lamb who is worthy (5:12). We will be reunited with our believing loved ones who died before us (Matthew 8:11).

According to Habermas, we will be able to grow in knowledge and truth, "thereby increasing our awareness of God and his works." Peter Kreeft writes that when we get to heaven, we will begin "the endless and endlessly fascinating task of exploring, learning, and loving the facets of infinity, the inexhaustible nature of God." We will not be omniscient—that is, we won't know everything—but we will continue to learn throughout eternity: things about heaven, about each other, and about God. Larry Richards writes:

> The Book of Revelation, in harmony with the rest of the New Testament and the Old, affirms the uniqueness of human beings. Created in God's image, no individual's identity can be simply snuffed out. Each of us is destined to remain ourselves, self-conscious and aware, for all eternity. For the lost, this means eternal punishment. For the saved, what it means is sketched in Revelation 21 and 22.

A New Heaven and a New Earth (Revelation 21:1-9)

As Revelation 21 opens, John sees "a new heaven and a new earth." What does that mean? Theologians tell us that the old earth and heaven won't be completely destroyed, but rather regenerated. The process will begin during the Millennium and will be completed after the Millennium and the Great White Throne judgment. Not only will the universe be restored to its original perfect splendor and harmony, but the human condition will be made perfect as well. We will experience no more death or sorrow or crying or pain. Truly God will make all things new.

The Holy City (Revelation 21:10-27)

Did you know that heaven will include a city? It's called the New Jerusalem. This is the section in Revelation that gives us the idea of the streets of heaven being paved with gold and the gates of heaven being made of pearls. Surely the New Jerusalem is a literal city, probably the city that Abraham hoped for:

> *Abraham...was confidently looking forward to a city with eternal foundations, a city designed and built by God* (Hebrews 11:10).

It's also the city that *we* long for:

> *For this world is not our home; we are looking forward to our city in heaven, which is yet to come* (Hebrews 13:14).

Will Everyone Fit?

Revelation 21 lists the dimensions of the Holy City: "In fact, it was in the form of a cube, for its length and width and height were each 1,400 miles." These dimensions could be symbolic, showing us that heaven will hold all of God's people. However, Anne Graham Lotz quotes a Bible scholar who estimated that 20 billion people could live in a cube this large with each person having a private 75-acre mansion.

This city is heaven, but it's not all of heaven. Think of the New Jerusalem as the capital city of heaven. The Bible doesn't specify but seems to indicate that we will be able to go throughout the new earth, which itself will be the center of a vast universe. Heaven will have no need for the sun, "for the glory of God illuminates the city, and the Lamb is its light" (Revelation 21:23). The description is almost more than we can comprehend. That's why the apostle Paul wrote:

> *No eye has seen, nor ear has heard, and no mind has imagined what God has prepared for those who love him* (1 Corinthians 2:9).

Images of Heaven

We may not be able to comprehend these truths and heaven may be beyond our imaginations, but we can still think about what heaven will be like. Gary Habermas presents five images from the Bible that help us to see what our experience in heaven might be like:

- We will have complete *peace* (Psalm 23:1-3).

- We will have complete *rest* (Psalm 91:1).

- We will have complete *security* and *protection* (Psalm 91:2).

- We will have complete *beauty* (Psalm 50:2).

- We will have complete *fellowship* (Matthew 26:29).

We've come to the end of our study on Revelation with a beautiful chapter that leaves us with a description of heaven, a final promise from Jesus, and an encouragement to expect the Lord's return.

Revelation Ends As Genesis Began (Revelation 22:1-6)

The Bible opened with Paradise. Because of sin, Paradise was lost. Now, as the Bible closes, God has remade the world. Paradise has been regained. Just as the Garden of Eden included a river and a tree of life, the tree of life in heaven is fed by the "pure river with the water of life" (22:1). God will finally satisfy our spiritual thirst (22:17). With no sin or evil in heaven, we will be able to freely eat from the tree of life.

We will finally see God face-to-face. No one has seen God's face since Adam and Eve sinned. God told Moses, "But you may not look directly at my face, for no one may see me and live" (Exodus 33:20). In heaven, God will fulfill what Jesus promised: "God blesses those whose hearts are pure, for they will see God" (Matthew 5:8). Night will never come in heaven, and we won't need any light, for God will be our light. And we will "reign forever and ever." This is the glorious promise of Revelation.

A Final Promise (Revelation 22:7-16)

The words of Jesus are both a comfort and a warning:

*Look, I am coming soon! Blessed are those who obey
the prophecy written in this scroll* (Revelation 22:7).

The word *soon* here means "imminent." That means
the definite return of Christ could happen at any time. To
those who know the Lord personally, that is a wonderful
thought. To those who continue to reject God, it is a
warning to repent while there is still time.

A Final Encouragement (Revelation 22:17-21)

John encourages us to live with an attitude of expec-
tancy. "Amen! Come, Lord Jesus!" he says. What does this
mean for us? We need to have a healthy view of the future
by being *ready, wise,* and *watchful.*

Be ready. You never know what's going to happen in
the world. We live in uncertain times. And you certainly
never know what's going to happen to you. As the Bible
says:

*How do you know what will happen tomorrow? For
your life is like the morning fog—it's here a little
while, then it's gone* (James 4:14).

Even if Jesus does not come in your lifetime, you will
meet Jesus when your life ends, and no one knows when
that day will come. We need to be ready.

Be wise. You don't need to fear the future, but you do
need to be concerned about living for God right now. The
Bible says:

*So be careful how you live, not as fools but as those
who are wise. Make the most of every opportunity for
doing good in these evil days. Don't act thought-
lessly, but try to understand what the Lord wants
you to do* (Ephesians 5:15-17).

Be watchful. Just as you wouldn't want a thief to break into your house when you were physically asleep, you don't want your life or the world to end when you are spiritually asleep. Jesus was very specific on this subject:

> *Watch out! Don't let me find you living in careless ease and drunkenness, and filled with the worries of this life. Don't let that day catch you unaware, as in a trap. For that day will come upon everyone living on the earth. Keep a constant watch* (Luke 21:34-35).

■ ▨ ▨

$\mathcal{S}$tudy the $\mathcal{W}$ord

1. How does believing in a literal heaven impact the way you live your life on earth now?

   Why don't Christians talk or sing about heaven very much these days?

2. In Revelation 21:2, the new Jerusalem is described as a "beautiful bride prepared for her husband." Who is the husband?

With that in mind, read Revelation 21:11-14. What imagery do you think of when you read this description of the New Jerusalem?

3. In Revelation 21:3, the voice from the throne says, "Look, the home of God is now among his people! He will live with them, and they will be his people. God himself will be with them." What does that mean to you?

4. What is missing in heaven? Why aren't these things needed?

5. Who are the first five people you want to meet and talk to when you get to heaven? Why these five?

6. Make a list of some additional comparisons and contrasts between Genesis and Revelation.

7. Write down one thing you can do to be ready, one thing you can do to be wise, and one thing you can do to be watchful.

Dig Deeper

*W*henever we write a book about God and His Word, we do a lot of research and reading. Here are the main books we used to write this study on Revelation. If you want to dig deeper into Revelation and the Bible, here's a great place to start.

Commentaries

Max Anders is the editor of an excellent series called the Holman New Testament Commentary. The volume on *Revelation* by Kendell Easley is excellent.

One of our favorite New Testament Bible scholars is William Barclay. He's down to earth yet deep (a rare combination). We used his two-volume book, *The Revelation of John,* from The Daily Study Bible Series.

J. Vernon McGee is another great Bible teacher. We relied on the three-volume *Revelation* from his Thru-The-Bible Commentary Series.

The Life Application Bible Commentary series is outstanding, and *Revelation* was a big help.

The NIV Application Commentary on *Revelation* by Craig S. Keener is very comprehensive and (you guessed it) practical.

The New Testament volume of *The Bible Knowledge Commentary,* edited by John Walvoord and Roy Zuck, provides valuable background and historical information.

Likewise, the New Testament volume of *The Bible Background Commentary* by Lawrence Richards is a great Bible study tool.

One of the best Bible commentary sets is the Expositor's Bible Commentary. We used Volume 12, which includes *Revelation* by Alan F. Johnson.

General Bible Study Helps

We wrote two books on the Bible we found helpful in writing our study. Check out *Knowing the Bible 101* and *Bruce & Stan's Guide to Bible Prophecy.* They are written in the same "user-friendly" style as this book.

Understanding the historical background is important when studying any Bible book. For Revelation we recommend Merrill Tenney's *New Testament Survey.*

Bible Translations

Obviously you can't study Revelation or the Bible without the primary source—the Bible! People often ask us, "Which Bible translation should I use?" We recommend that your primary study Bible be a *literal* translation (as opposed to a paraphrase), such as the *New International Version* (NIV) of the Bible or the *New American Standard Bible* (NASB). However, using a Bible paraphrase, such as *The Living Bible* or *The Message* is perfectly acceptable in your devotional reading.

Our personal choice is the *New Living Translation* (NLT), a Bible translation that uses a method called "dynamic equivalence." This means that the scholars who translated the Bible from the original languages (Hebrew and Greek) used a "thought-for-thought" translation philosophy rather than a "word-for-word" approach. It's just as accurate but easier to read. In the final analysis, the Bible that's best for you is the Bible you enjoy reading because you can understand it.

A Word About Personal Pronouns

When we write about God, we prefer to capitalize all personal pronouns that refer to God, Jesus, and the Holy Spirit. These would include *He, Him, His,* and *Himself.* However, not all writers follow this practice, and nothing is wrong with that. In fact, personal pronouns for God were not capitalized in the original languages, which is why you'll find that the Bible uses *he, him, his,* and *himself.*

Bruce and Stan would enjoy hearing from you. Contact them with your questions, comments, or to schedule them to speak at an event.

Snail mail: Twelve Two Media
PO Box 25997
Fresno, CA 93729-5997

E-mail: info@twelvetwomedia.com

Web site: www.twelvetwomedia.com

Exclusive Online Feature

Here's a Bible study feature you're really going to like!
Simply go online at:

www.christianity101online.com

There you'll find a website designed exclusively for users of the Christianity 101 Bible Studies series. Just click on the book you are studying, and you will discover additional information, resources, and helps, including:

- *Background Material*—We can't put everything in this Bible study, so this online section includes more material, such as historical, geographical, theological, and biographical information.

- *More Questions*—Do you need more questions for your Bible study? Here are additional questions for each chapter. Bible study leaders will find this especially helpful.

- *Answers to Your Questions*—Do you have a question about something in your Bible study? Post your question and an "online scholar" will respond.

- *FAQ's*—In this section are answers to some of the more frequently asked questions about the book you are studying.

What are you waiting for? Go online and become a part of the Christianity 101 community!

Knowing the Bible 101

With their fresh, contemporary perspective, Bruce and Stan provide an overview of the origin, themes, and context of the Bible; pack in maps, references, and learning aids; and include a three-month study plan.

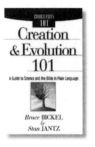

Creation and Evolution 101

With their distinctively winsome style, Bruce Bickel and Stan Jantz explore the essentials of creation and evolution and offer fascinating evidence of God's hand at work. Perfect for individual or group use.

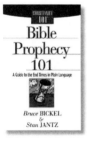

Bible Prophecy 101

In their contemporary, down-to-earth way, Bruce and Stan present the Bible's answers to your end-times questions. You will appreciate their helpful explanations of the rapture, the tribulation, the millennium, Christ's second coming, and other important topics.

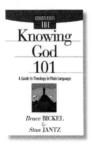

Knowing God 101

This book is brimming with joy! Whatever your background, you will love the inspiring descriptions of God's nature, personality, and activities. You will also find straightforward responses to the essential questions about God.

Christianity 101™ Bible Studies

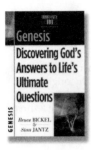

Genesis: Discovering God's Answers to Life's Ultimate Questions

"In the beginning" says it all. Genesis sets the stage for the drama of human history. This guide gives you a good start and makes sure you don't get lost along the way.

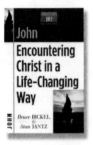

John: Encountering Christ in a Life-Changing Way

This study reveals who Jesus is by demonstrating the dramatic changes He made in the lives of the people he met, including Nicodemus, the woman at the well, Lazarus, and John, "the disciple whom Jesus loved."

Acts: Living in the Power of the Holy Spirit

Bruce and Stan offer a fresh look at the ongoing ministry of Jesus through the church. They highlight the drama of the early Christians' triumph over darkness and their explosive growth from a band of 120 fearful followers to a thriving, worldwide church.

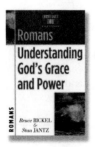

Romans: Understanding God's Grace and Power

Paul's letter to the church in Rome is his clearest explanation and application of the good news. This fresh new study of Romans assures you that the gospel is God's answer to every human need.

Christianity 101™ Bible Studies

1 & 2 Corinthians: Finding Your Unique Place in God's Plan

This enlightening study explores the apostle Paul's helpful responses to issues that churches continue to face today: maintaining unity in the church, exercising spiritual gifts, and identifying authentic Christian ministry.

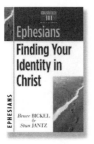

Ephesians: Finding Your Identity in Christ

Verse for verse, the book of Ephesians is one of the most profound, powerful, and practical books in the Bible. This guide reveals the heart of Paul's teaching on the believer's identity in Christ.

Philippians/Colossians: Experiencing the Joy of Knowing Christ

This new 13-week study of two of Paul's most intimate letters will inspire you to know Christ more intimately and maintain your passion and vision. Filled with helpful background information, up-to-date applications, and penetrating, open-ended questions.

Revelation: Unlocking the Mysteries of the End Times

Have you ever read the final chapters of the Scriptures, only to finish with more questions than answers? Bruce and Stan help you understand Revelation's encouraging message and apply it to your life today.